THE PATTERN OF CHINESE HISTORY

Cycles, Development, or Stagnation?

PROBLEMS IN ASIAN CIVILIZATIONS

UNDER THE EDITORIAL DIRECTION OF THE COMMITTEE ON ORIENTAL STUDIES, COLUMBIA UNIVERSITY

EDITORIAL COMMITTEE: *Wm. Theodore de Bary*, COLUMBIA UNIVERSITY • *Ainslie T. Embree*, COLUMBIA UNIVERSITY • *John Meskill*, BARNARD COLLEGE • *Johanna M. Menzel*, VASSAR COLLEGE • *Arthur Tiedemann*, THE CITY COLLEGE OF NEW YORK

PROBLEMS IN ASIAN CIVILIZATION

THE PATTERN
OF CHINESE HISTORY

Cycles, Development, or Stagnation?

EDITED WITH AN INTRODUCTION BY

John Meskill

BARNARD COLLEGE

D. C. HEATH AND COMPANY · BOSTON

Library of Congress Catalog Card Number 65-17466

Copyright © 1965 by D. C. Heath and Company

BOSTON   ENGLEWOOD   CHICAGO   DALLAS   SAN FRANCISCO   ATLANTA   LONDON   TORONTO

PRINTED IN THE UNITED STATES OF AMERICA
PRINTED APRIL 1965

Table of Contents

Introduction

STUDENTS sometimes praise the length of Chinese history, as if the longer the history the better. Yet length may breed more indifference than interest if the history appears to be only a vast collection of unrelated events. Chinese history becomes interesting when its facts are untangled and a pattern revealed. One way to do that is to divide the history up into periods. However, the question has long been, what scheme of periods helps explain the history best? This question has not only divided historians in ancient China, Western scholars, and modern Asian historians but even unexpectedly entered modern political disputes.

I. EARLY CHINESE VIEWS

Early in China, men formed views of a dominant pattern of history. First, the past had held a Golden Age, when all men lived in harmony and peace. In time this Age of Grand Unity gave way to the striving of men against each other. Systems of government and principles of conduct became necessary to regulate selfish, sequestering, destructive habits. In that sense the age after the Age of Grand Unity began history, when mankind's degenerate behavior set in motion the familiar processes of change, such as the rise and fall of kings and the victories and defeats of armies. Yet the standards by which later times would be evaluated remained those of the Golden Age: unity, order and a world for all to share. Second, changes that marked post-Unity history were seen to follow a cyclical, not a lineal, course. Events of nature — the succession of the seasons, the alternation of night and day, and the phases of the moon, for example — contributed to the idea that all events passed through cycles. At bottom, the process was the eternal succession of the Five Agents — wood, fire, earth, metal, and water — the elemental forces of nature. Somewhat

like the application in the West at times of natural laws to social events, the theory of a natural cycle began to be used shortly before the beginning of the Christian era to explain the succession of political dynasties, seen as moving in correspondence to the changes of the elemental agents.

Practice and custom strengthened the idea that the dynasty formed a period in the cycle of history. An early historian, Pan Ku (32–92 A.D.), justified writing the history of only one dynasty on the grounds that one man was capable of that and no more. It became customary for one dynasty to compile an official or standard history of the previous dynasty. Though the official histories eventually became the work of committees, undermining Pan Ku's argument of the ability of one man, the state gave the practice such strength that the single dynasty became the prevalent period of history in early times.

The first selections of this book provide early statements of the idea of the Age of Grand Unity and what followed and of the idea of the cycle as an explanation of historical events, illustrated in the words of Ssu-ma Ch'ien (145 B.C.?–90 B.C.?), himself a pillar of the school of continuous history. The idea of cyclical motion came to influence so many aspects of history that no one early document illustrates them all. We have added a brief résumé of some of the generalizations about Chinese society which became associated with the cycle by a modern scholar, Professor Arthur F. Wright.

Despite the domination of the one-dynasty approach, other views of the proper divisions of history never disappeared entirely. From early times the possibility of dividing history in other ways had been shown. The Age of Grand Unity itself may be one example of a non-dynastic period, meager though information of it is, and the Period of the Warring States

(403–221 B.C.), even though the name is borrowed from a book, is certainly one. Each period is defined by characteristics, namely unity or order and war or disorder, rather than by a dynasty or any particular institution. The standards of unity and disunity (or order and disorder), whether measuring a dynasty or an age, appear so central to the traditional methods of periodization that we shall recall them as a Chinese leitmotiv when we examine the outlook of European scholars. Another kind of periodic division appears in the reign-name, it, too, a description, or perhaps a magical prescription, of the character of a period; for example, *Yung-lo*, "Perpetual Happiness" (the reign from 1403 to 1424).

The view, however, that treatment of a single dynasty failed to promote the fullest understanding of history owed most to the early work of Ssu-ma Ch'ien, *Records of the Grand Historian* (*Shih chi*). Carrying the story of Chinese government from the earliest accounts to his own age, Ssu-ma Ch'ien, though he offered no explicit alternative scheme of periods and tended to organize his book by dynasties, established by the scope and quality of his work the ideal of comprehensive history.

Later scholars, especially in the Sung dynasty (960–1279), referred frequently to Ssu-ma Ch'ien in support of their arguments for viewing history at length. Some of them, such as Ssu-ma Kuang (1019–1086), author of the *General Mirror for the Aid of Government* (*Tzu-chih t'ung-chien*), emulated him. Others, such as the three men represented here — Lü Tsu-ch'ien (1137–1181), Cheng Ch'iao (1108–1166), and Ma Tuan-lin (thirteenth century) — questioned more or less directly the adequacy of the one-dynasty period. As a product of their studies, views of history as a process turning on certain fateful organizational changes emerged in late traditional times. They are represented in this book by selections from Huang Tsung-hsi (1610–1695) and Ku Yen-wu (1613–1682).

Brief illustrations of such views indicate not that the idea of history in cycles ever weakened decisively but that Chinese historical thought vigorously continued to oppose submitting the record of the past to any one mold. Other efforts that cannot readily be illustrated should at least be mentioned, since they qualify further the domination of the one-dynasty view. The topical form of history (*chi-shih pen-mo*), for example, though usually cast within the bounds of a single dynasty, narrating events in terms of development and denouement, shows no necessary cyclical impulse. The T'ang historiographer Liu Chih-chi (661–721) suggested a periodization — high antiquity, middle antiquity, recent antiquity, and the modern age — which, at least in its terms, indicated a view of history proceeding, indeed, "descending," lineally in some sense. In the concern, evident in the works of many historians, for unity and disunity, often almost synonymous for order and disorder, appears a theme that, although suggesting a cycle, releases it from its dynastic bounds and makes possible periods that go beyond or fall short of the duration of a dynasty.

Chinese historiography, capable of conceiving of a number of periodic patterns, did not rigidly hold to the dynasty as the only useful period when China's scholars turned their attention to Western periodization. The idea of a cycle, however, persisted tenaciously in practice, sometimes in such modern dress as to belie its age.

II. WORLD HISTORY FROM THE WEST

In modern times European currents of thought have affected Chinese historiography, even though the full measure of the force is still uncertain. Our concern here must be with only one element, the thought of Europeans who have attempted to see history on a large scale. It would be impossible, of course, to speak of all who have discussed China. Most regrettable is the difficulty of representing in this book much original Western history of China, since Western scholars of Chinese history have paid little attention so far to periodization.

The selections stress "world" history, a philosophy that attempts to explain all history everywhere. World history at first contributes to the periodization of Chinese history only indirectly, but eventually affects some of the most vigorously proposed recent schemes.

Modern knowledge of China began to accumulate in Europe from the sixteenth century, when not only China but other great parts of Asia long out of touch with Europe and, of course, the New World came within reach of European discoverers. From the eighteenth century, Europeans, beginning with Voltaire, began to write histories meant to inform men not only of the European past but of the non-European as well. One result in the succeeding two centuries, especially apparent in the selections here, has been a tendency to find patterns and movements universal in human experience and even susceptible of analysis into single entities or forces working throughout all history.

G. W. F. Hegel, the first writer represented in this section, gave Europe the idea of a world history advancing in a line across space and upwards through time. He saw history making a world-spanning progress, beginning in China and moving west with the sun to Europe in his day. History, the story of the growth of self-conscious Reason, whose object is Freedom (meaning approximately a sense of self-determination), was born in China, where only One Power, the Sovereign, was free. Thereafter, the consciousness of freedom moved westward until the idea that all were free came to maturity in Europe. Meanwhile, back in China life went on unhistorically, changing restlessly without advance, passing through a repetitive circle of decline and subsidence. Hegel suffered, no doubt, from the limited European knowledge of China in his day, but his interpretation of history as the progress of an abstract metaphysical essence, the Idea, toward its destiny of fulfillment beyond China has stimulated later European views. His suggestion that history had run its course, its essence achieving embodiment in Europe and fulfillment in the absolute consciousness of freedom, may also have contributed in an indirect way to the deterministic quality of the most famous "post-Hegelian," Karl Marx.

Marx, who wrote nothing on China suitable for inclusion in the selections, nevertheless demands attention, if only for the schemes developed in his name. He reflects much of Hegel and other Europeans, seeing history as a progress toward a superior condition of mankind and viewing Asia as the backwater of history and Europe as its mainstream.

His brief references to an "Asiatic method of production," the first of the "epochs in the progress of the economic formation of society," [1] suggest, though his intention has been debated, that he has followed both Hegel's picture of a universal progress of history across the face of the earth and the ascription to Asia of changelessness. But his major innovation consciously contradicted Hegel by maintaining that the roots of the forms of society lie in material conditions of life, not in the progress of the mind.

That Marx wrote little on China herself has given rise to different opinions of what his scattered remarks signified, generating debates that persist to the present time. Some of his comments on Asia (he tended to speak of Asia indiscriminately, although Hegel had made distinctions of a sort) illustrate a view like Hegel's of the unchanging East. The key to all phenomena in the East, he wrote, for example — referring to Turkey, Persia, and northern India, the last being the source of many of his observations — was the absence of private property in land. Instead, Asia characteristically came under powerful, central-

[1] That, at least, is one of the interpretations of his statement, "In broad outlines we can designate the Asiatic, the ancient, the feudal, and the modern bourgeois methods of production as so many epochs in the progress of the economic formation of society." See Karl Marx and Friedrich Engels, *Basic Writing on Politics and Philosophy.* Ed. by Lewis S. Feuer (Anchor Books), p. 44.

ized governments — Oriental or Asiatic despotisms — whose interference through public works, notably artificial irrigation systems, contributed to keeping their societies static and miserable from the remotest antiquity.

In general, Marx stimulated two impulses in the periodization of Chinese history. One of them arose from the view he shared with other Europeans of a society lacking unprecedented, essential innovation that would give its history a lineal or progressive form. Historians under that impulse would find Chinese history made up mainly of one long period, if the term period remained significant at all. The characteristic institution of the period would be a heavily dominant government. Society would not have progressed into new patterns, such as occurred subsequently in Europe.

The second impulse lies in the universality of the Marxian view. Provided the Asiatic method of production be understood as not standing first in an inexorable sequence of methods, the universality of the remaining ancient, feudal, and modern bourgeois methods of production might envelope Chinese history as well as any other. This impulse, to see Chinese history as one expression of universal history, has dominated Communist discussions of China. A special Asiatic method of production, once debated among Communist theoreticians and still crucial to some social scientists, both Communist and non-Communist, has received little attention in authoritative Soviet statements for some time. "Five *main* types of relations of production are known to history: primitive communal, slave, feudal, capitalist and Socialist." [2] The Chinese Communist Party for its part rejected in 1928 the argument that China was an Asiatic society. Working from Marx's theory of social epochs, they divide Chinese history into five periods, of which the middle three — slave, feudal, and capitalist or some offshoot of capitalist, such as semi-colonial — attract the most attention.

Hegel and Marx illustrate another way of thought involved in modern approaches to Chinese history. It is the notion that the central questions of history concern power, the chance, in Max Weber's definition, "of a man or of a number of men to realize their own will in a communal action even against the resistance of others who are participating in the action." [3] For Marxists, of course, the power of one class over others to control the system of material production becomes the major theme; but power shapes the thought of other European theorists as well. Early Chinese historians never ignored power. They tended, however, to notice the effect of power on social order more than to analyze and define the sources of power and struggles for it.

Not all Europeans who have written on world history have fitted China into a comprehensive progressive scheme. Oswald Spengler, for example, put forth a view in the selection following Hegel's, that seems at first somewhat like the Chinese idea of cycle. As difficult as it is to represent the core of his views, which have been called impressionistic and fantastic in recent times, he clearly conceives of a cycle when he speaks of history as the repeated expression of a limited number of forms. The idea of a series of periods, recurring each time with the same duration in culture after culture, seems kindred to a Chinese view of natural and regular periodicity. Yet Spengler used different concepts. If for the Chinese the true paradigm of historical movements was the natural universe, for Spengler it was the living organism. To the Chinese, history was as endless as the world, but to Spengler it was as mortal as a plant. Its movement followed a life-cycle, not a cosmic cycle. When history died, what was left was a

[2] *History of the Communist Party of the Soviet Union* (Bolsheviks), *Short Course,* ed. by a Commission of the Central Committee of the C.P.S.U. (B.) (New York: International Publishers, 1939), p. 123.

[3] Max Weber. *From Max Weber: Essays in Sociology,* tr. H. H. Gerth and C. Wright Mills. Galaxy Book, 1958, p. 180.

fossil, in his terms a civilization, the petrified form of a once living culture. Sharing an idea that others had expressed before him, he found Chinese history to have ended long ago. What followed was existence without history.

In another respect Spengler expressed a European approach. He found that the history of every culture followed a sequence of epochs toward the fulfillment of the Idea of *the* Culture, the ideal primitive culture-form. The form of Chinese history being an expression of one Idea, or universal abstract essence, it shared with all other histories one general course, which was determined by a force independent of historical facts.

Arnold Toynbee, represented next in the selections, rejected the cyclical view of history as paramount, finding instead a rhythmical, irreversible movement that turns like a wheel across the ground. Nevertheless, he repeated and reinforced themes that other Europeans, including Spengler, shared. He found, for example, that all civilizations suggested a similar purpose. The idea of purpose in civilizations, though apparently religious in Professor Toynbee's view, resembles Spengler's more organic "fulfillment" of a culture. For both men, history moved toward an end and might reach it though the society that was its host continued to exist afterwards. Chinese history had ended for Spengler early in the Christian era; it ended, as the main story of Far Eastern Society, for Professor Toynbee in approximately the fourteenth century, after which Chinese society continued on in "petrifaction." Like Spengler, Professor Toynbee seemed to see history, if the term denotes essential change or development, as a process that may cease to exist in a society. The idea of historyless society, unconceived in Chinese thought, finds a place in a number of European theories.

III. MODERN CYCLICAL INTERPRETATIONS

When Chinese historians of older times discussed events as symptoms of a cyclical process, they usually concentrated on the conduct of affairs at court. Especially the character and actions of the emperor and those closest to him seemed to explain the course of the dynasty. True, events outside the court — the state of mind and of the economy of the people, for example, and even the appearance of omens and portents in nature — also gave signs of the times. Theoretically, however, notable events outside the court signified or expressed order or disorder; they were parts, not primary causes, of a process. The primary causes lay in the court and the morality of its work.

New European explanations of history have often taken a different approach. Sometimes they have shown the Chinese past in such a different light that its whole shape appears changed, even to the disappearance of cycles. At other times, they seem to have permitted the idea of the cycle, differently described, to persist. When that happens, one change is the discovery of new ways of identifying the cycle. A second, implied in the first, is an extension of the signs of the cycle beyond the sphere of the imperial court and its events. A third is the understanding of the cycle as a manifold universal pattern, and a fourth a consideration of the cycle within a lineal view of history.

In the first modern selection, for example, J. S. Lee attempts to apply to history a method of analysis that grew and proved fruitful among the natural sciences of the West. He tries to discover discrete events of a single class — "internecine wars" — and, by measuring the frequency of the events, the number of internecine wars occurring within a fixed period of time, to provide a chart of the "general state of national existence," or, in the older terms, periods of order and disorder. The history of China may then be characterized by the quantity of one element, "defiant force," within it. The pattern that emerges follows a regular cycle of periods of approximately eight hundred years each. Western analytical methods that have shown much order in nature appear here to support a Chinese idea that mankind is part of a naturalistic system. Although Mr. Lee does not try to explain what governs the regularity of the events he examines, he suggests that the "force of nature" must be considered.

At the same time that his essay shows a way of applying methods derived from the natural sciences to history, it suggests one of the difficulties in doing so. That is the difficulty of classifying historical events by universally acceptable definitions. Mr. Lee, for example, classifies the Chin and Manchu invasions of China proper as internecine wars — by his definition, wars between peoples of Chinese civilization — and the Mongol invasion as not internecine. Other scholars have argued that all the invasions belong together, classified as foreign conquests, depriving the discussion of agreement on basic definitions of the kind that supports research in the natural sciences.

The dynasty itself still looks cyclical to some modern scholars, even though other periods may take precedence. The new statement of the dynastic cycle comes mainly from Western writers or others trained in Western methods. It appears in an early description by Professor Karl A. Wittfogel as a pattern of political fortune no longer set by the morality of the court but by economic and political movements governing the span of a dynasty.

The ruling official class, which as representative of the commonwealth struggled against the feudal land rent on behalf of the state form of land tax, saw itself confronted by new opposing forces. Because the latter were linked by necessity to the new society, they were not so easy to get rid of as the outmoded old ones. A vicious economic-political circle resulted: accumulation of private wealth of the new type and accumulation of private possession of land in the hands of officials, "gentry" and great merchants, reduction of land tax, enfeebling of the state, agrarian crisis — invasions — state crisis. Although this vicious circle could be periodically smoothed over by the fall and rise of "dynasties," it could never really be overcome.[4]

Other scholars have elaborated the thesis. Professor Edwin O. Reischauer prefaces his statement of an economic-administrative cycle with a description of the symptoms of the cycle in the court, reminding us of the central concern of the Chinese in the past. Instead of a cycle dependent on the morality of emperors and officials, however, he sees an invariable degeneration of society through the psycho-biological weaknesses of the emperors and a struggle for power among rival factions.

In the Western train of thought the cycle becomes a secondary element of periodization. For Professor Wittfogel the cycle is a component within the more general theme of an essentially fixed structure of power. For Professor Reischauer the cycle seems to be a secondary pattern within larger evolutionary movements.

Lest the subordination of the dynasty to other historical patterns seem to discount it as an incubus of traditional Chinese ideas, we should remember that at least in a strictly political sense the dynasty was a distinct historical period. As such, the course of government dynasty by dynasty deserves closer analysis, to see whether a cycle of government appears. Professor Lien-sheng Yang has suggested traditional and modern categories and definitions in need of study or clarification. If they are clarified, he implies, the study of Chinese history as a whole should benefit, whether or not a cycle is demonstrated.

Comparable in novelty to J. S. Lee's use of statistics to define periods is H. T. Lei's attempt in the following selection to relate Chinese history to a worldwide pattern. He, too, begins with a cycle of history, the period of "classical" China from the beginning to A.D. 383, defined primarily in terms of the degree of political unification. The significant field of events, however, has broadened to cover the world, or at least the Mediterranean, European, Indian, and Chinese regions, for he finds the course followed by "classical" China to fit a uni-

---

[4] K. A. Wittfogel, "The Foundations and Stages of Chinese Economic History," *Zeitschrift für Sozialforschung* IV (Paris, 1935), pp. 52–53.

versal sequence of political orders: tribal — feudal — state — imperial. Each order, moreover, lasts everywhere approximately the same length of time. Such is the appeal of the pattern that where it is not seen, he says, the loss of historical material has obscured it.

Mr. Lei's second period, Tartar-Buddhist China (from 383 to the present), although he calls it, too, a cycle, differs from a cycle as understood earlier in that it shows no repetition of the sequence of orders of the past. To the contrary, it is politically unchanging, though "culturally" creative. Apparently, despite the use of the word cycle, a radically different idea dominates, for between the first and second periods the same events do not recur. History has entered not a second phase of a cycle; it

has entered an unprecedented phase. Moreover, the phase has no analogue elsewhere, for only China has passed through it. The second cycle, to keep his term, is approaching its end, and the coming third cycle, which will be one of world empire, suggests that the cycle idea, rather than having been wholly abandoned, could be raised to the level of a world process. The sequence from tribes through feudalism and statehood to empire in particular regions of the world could appear again in the ordering of the world as a whole. Mr. Lei's interest in establishing universal patterns of history and predicting the shape of the future, as well as the recasting of Chinese history to introduce noncyclical change, bespeaks the force of European ideas.

CHART OF THE THREE AGES [IN THE EVOLUTION] OF UNITING THE NATIONS INTO ONE WORLD

1. The Age of Disorder at the Time the First Foundations of One World are Laid.	The Age of Increasing Peace-and-Equality, When One World is Gradually Coming into Being.	The Age of Complete Peace-and-Equality When One World has been Achieved.
2. The old states are allied.	New public states are created.	There are no states, [only] the world.
9. All the states have monarchs or presidents . . .	Most of the states have presidents, [although] a few may have monarchs . . . under the control of the public government.	. . . There are only [local] presidents . . . under the control of the public government.

IV. MODERN LINEAL THEORIES

Some of the Europeans we have mentioned spoke of China on the basis of little or wrong evidence and never from a knowledge of the literature as broad as that of Eastern historians. Nevertheless, some European concepts of history when they reached the East gained a hearing and, far from being wholly rejected, were more or less adroitly adopted. The process, which was bound up with larger questions of the confrontation between East and West, followed no simple course. Scholars are only gradually coming to understand the manner in which Western ideas became accepted and interpreted by Chinese whose premises and viewpoints had been formed in a different tradition. The study of individual thinkers, each subject to a welter of

influences, would be beyond us here. Nevertheless, without knowing the stages of thought that led to the conclusions we see, we should outline here the schemes, which could not be included in the selections, of two early spokesmen for modernization, K'ang Yu-wei (1858–1927) and Liang Ch'i-ch'ao (1873–1929). Both accepted ideas that were to be taken up by more recent writers.

K'ang's periodization, embracing not only the past but also the future, emerges from his book *The Grand Unity (Ta t'ung shu)*. Small portions of the chart in the book suggest the whole.[5]

[5] K'ang Yu-wei. *Ta T'ung Shu: The One-World Philosophy of K'ang Yu-wei.* Tr. Laurence G. Thompson (London, George Allen and Unwin, 1958), pp. 105–121.

Clearly, elements of an old Chinese approach remain: the term Grand Unity itself and the idea of the three ages have classical roots. Even the most general characteristics of the ages, degrees of disorder or order and of disunity or unity, represent a Chinese emphasis. Yet the innovations stand out. History moves in a progress toward a superior human condition, plainly a communist Utopia. Though K'ang argued his scheme from Confucian precedents, his followers insisted that he envisioned the stages as irreversible, not in the traditional cycle. The stages occur, moreover, universally.

K'ang's pupil, Liang Ch'i-ch'ao, accepts another European viewpoint. His periodization concerns China directly, not China as one in a world of nations moving in step toward harmony. Even so, he follows, apparently out of expediency, the conventional European divisions: ancient, medieval, and modern. He calls China's ancient period, from the beginnings to the unification under the Ch'in dynasty (221–207 B.C.), "China in China": a period of the self-development, mutual competition, and self-organization of the Chinese people. The medieval period, from the Ch'in dynasty to the end of the Ch'ien-lung reign (1736–1795), is "China in Asia": a period when the Chinese people come into touch and competition with Asia's peoples. Power becomes centralized, leading to the completion of an autocratic political structure. (Elsewhere, Liang writes of the lack of significant political and social change in China ever since the Ch'in dynasty.) China dominates her neighbors spiritually. Finally, the modern period is that of "China in the world," when China and all the Asian peoples come into touch and competition with the West. Chinese political forms begin to change.[6]

Liang has turned from his master's rather metaphysical view of common progress everywhere to a view much closer to the European cast of mind that looks to power. He no longer speaks of history as a ques-

tion of order and disorder. It is a struggle, each nation against the others, in which the fittest survive. In accepting a Social-Darwinist attitude, Liang takes a giant step away from his Chinese fathers. From a history explained by the morality of the rulers he sees one explained by competition to survive; from the model of the natural universe he turns to the model of the living organism. If Chinese attitudes still lie beneath his statements, his brief essay gives no hint of them.

Conceivably both K'ang Yu-wei and Liang Ch'i-ch'ao, as men intricately involved in political action to modernize China, reflect a greater absorption of European thinking than men more wholly given to scholarship, even though Liang, at least, stands among the principal modern Chinese scholars. Their periodizations, not very closely argued, seem meant as much to guide action in the future as to explain the past. Yet among professional East Asian historians, too, European concepts have made a strong impression.

Japanese scholarly circles responded earlier on the whole than Chinese, and in Japan the modern periodization of Chinese history owes much to Naitō Konan (1866–1934). Naitō, before taking up a post in Kyoto University, had worked as a journalist and diplomat on the continent. He showed the greatest interest in China's modern political affairs and Japan's relationship to them, and his scholarship also reflects political concerns. Yet his reputation in academic circles approached legendary proportions. His knowledge of Chinese history was said to be encyclopedic, and his lectures drew students from as far away as Tokyo University.

In a number of essays and lectures he developed a periodization that has since been styled the Naitō hypothesis. "China" (_Shina-ron_),[7] an essay we have foregone for a later statement developed after him, introduces his starting point. Under the subtitle, "Monarchy or Republic?" he states the necessity of penetrating the spirit of

[6] Liang Ch'i-ch'ao. _Yin-ping-shih wen-chi_, Chunghua Shu-chü, ed., 34/24b, 25a.

[7] Naitō Konan. _Shina-ron_. Tokyo, Sōgen-sha, 1938, esp. 8–53.

history and transcending its details to answer the question whether China's future will be monarchical or republican. Historians, he says, when they mark off periods of high antiquity, middle antiquity, and modern times, do not mean them simply as times of relative distance from the present. Each has a characteristic content. In the Occident, the term "modern age" signifies a post-Renaissance rise in the power of the common people, or economic changes following the discovery of new lands, or changes in social organization. In China, too, he continues, periods can be established from the same point of view. Consideration of the modern age in terms of content and historical significance shows it reasonable to begin 800 to 1100 years back, in the time of mid-T'ang, the Five Dynasties, and Northern Sung (roughly A.D. 800–1100) periods.

He proceeds in this and other writings to describe fundamental changes in Chinese culture, sometimes exemplified as a change from an "aristocratic society" to an "autocratic" political form that occurred at that time, which marks the center of the hypothesis.

His thought makes some familiar assumptions. He begins by asking what form the future government of China will take. In neither East nor West, of course, is it novel to base predictions of the future on history. To the degree to which history seemed cyclical to Chinese of the past, however, the future would seem certain to repeat the past. Naitō, by introducing into his question a new term, republicanism, which the old Chinese cycle did not contain, suggests unprecedented change, an assumption of a lineal view of history. The view becomes clearer when he offers as an example a tripartite periodization, each period with a character of its own, although he does not propose that Chinese periods need be of the same number or carry the same names or characteristics as European periods. His stress on content marks an important contribution, for East Asian historians had tended in recent times to divide Chinese history into three periods on no

express grounds, apparently following the European order expediently. His stress also implies a fuller employment of historical facts to substantiate the periods than was apparent in the visionary scheme of K'ang Yu-wei or the abstract summation of Liang Ch'i-ch'ao. Like Liang, however, Naitō conveys a sense of connection between periodization and current political issues. Perhaps his emphasis on the modern period reflects a feeling that China stands at a critical point, possibly at the time of change from one period to another, touching the issue of periodization with political emotion.

This book contains, instead of a selection from his works, a more recent statement of periodization developed from Naitō's position. Professor Miyazaki Ichisada, a leading representative of the Kyoto school of sinology, proposes a four-fold division of Chinese history developing lineally. Not only does the lineal course suggest the influence of Europe; the first age in its imperial unity, the second in its disunity, and the fourth in its industrial culture also correspond to European ages. This common worldwide historical sequence, however, includes regional differences. The special aristocratic society of the second age in China differed radically from Europe's feudalism, and the Western industrial revolution abbreviated in Europe a period that in China enjoyed a long life. The third period, one of autocratic government, would seem to have found its model expression in China, not in Europe, where in places it never appeared.

The next exponent of progressive history in these selections, Professor Wolfram Eberhard, introduces his discussion of periods by saying that the European division of history into ancient, medieval, and modern periods is generally accepted as a "practical expedient as well as for internal reasons inherent in the different principles of classification." The acceptance of the originally European tripartite plan as expedient and the subsequent justification of it by argument have guided a number of writers on modern East Asia. Professor

Eberhard's emphasis on social classes as the keys to his scheme also illustrates how Western concepts have been applied to China. Thus antiquity is defined as the period of feudalism, the middle ages the period of gentry society, and the modern age the period of the formation of a middle class.

THE MARXIAN INFLUENCE

The decisive importance of economic power and class domination, suggested above by Professor Eberhard's terms, impressed Chinese writers strongly in the third and fourth decades of this century, when periodization became a topic of much discussion. In those decades, diversity of intellectual opinion may have been more characteristic than uniformity, but interpretations owing much to Marxism proved especially attractive, judging from numbers. They dominated what was called "the controversy on China's social history."

Ch'ao-ting Chi illustrates the idea of history governed by economics. Still seeing divisions of history according to the old themes of unity and disunity, he now explains periods in terms of control of economic resources. Over the alternating periods he places the mantle of one superperiod, from Ch'in times until the 19th century, when basic political and social forms underwent no essential change, despite shifts in the physical site of power. His plan shares with others in the book both the idea of a great division in Ch'in-Han times and a long, essential sameness thereafter. The great period he regards as "semi-feudal," a description evoking the modern Marxian use of the term to designate economic relationships that may exist without feudal political forms.

Next, a modern Japanese scholar, Maeda Naonori (1915–1949), proposes that history, though impelled by economic forces, may still conform to the Naitō hypothesis. Accepting as given the European-style tripartite progress, he finds that the ancient period of Chinese history ended in the T'ang dynasty (618–907) and that, moreover, the end of the ancient period in both Japan and Korea had a certain correlation to that of China, so that "Oriental history" seems marked everywhere by a "parallelism" of stages of development.

His periodization has tended to gain adherents among the Tokyo or "Historical Studies" school (named after the Historical Studies Society of Tokyo University), in rivalry with the Kyoto school. As Kyoto University's textbook *History of China* follows the Miyazaki periodization, so Tokyo University's *History of China* shows a periodization based on Maeda.

Maeda's discussion shows the tendency to see a "universal" history in one of the senses suggested before. His "Orient" undergoes as a unit the same sequence from ancient to medieval periods that occurred elsewhere, most notably in the Occident. His universality differs from Hegel's in that history does not move in space across the earth, from Spengler's in that it does not recur endlessly time after time, and from Chinese universality in that it has several centers that undergo the same periods more or less simultaneously.

Universality of a similar kind appears more explicitly in the selection by Professor Chien Po-tsan of the Academy of Sciences in Peking. The selection, without proposing a periodization of its own, reviews the discussion underway in mainland academic circles. All the historians whose views Professor Chien summarizes begin from the premise that Chinese history like all history passed through periods of slavery, feudalism, and (incipient) capitalism. The universal history, moreover, moves according to the "inner reality" of the power and relations of production, not primarily through such external phenomena as politics, law, and other systems. The search, however, still seems to seek certain essences rather than dominant functions. Thus, as Professor Chien notes, certain terms essential to the explanation of history, such as "farmer" and "private field," have yet to yield their essential historical significance.

V. ORIENTAL DESPOTISM

The next selection in the book presents the scheme of Professor Karl A. Wittfogel.

In much of his work, Professor Wittfogel has elaborated and extended the old European idea of an Oriental despotism into a theory of a type of society, no longer confined to Asia, of which China was a highly developed example. Certain basic conditions arising from the material environment, including the source of water, he proposes, led to the early formation of social features, most notably a "state stronger than society," that endured for millennia. His fundamental scheme of periods, — the simple hydraulic society, the semi-complex, and the complex —, although originally lineal in the European manner, shifts to another European view, that of the static East, from approximately the third century B.C., when China achieved the complex form of hydraulic society that characterized her until the nineteenth century. During the long period of complex hydraulic society, he says, Chinese history fell into subdivisions of typically Chinese and foreign conquest dynasties — as well as the dynastic cycle — but essential features of society, in which the state, the institution of greatest power, was most important, remained unchanged.

VI. REFLECTIONS AND RESERVATIONS OF HISTORIANS

None of the periodizations illustrated in this book has won general agreement among historians of China. To represent all the kinds of criticism would require more than a book; two critical statements, however, one on the purpose and methods of periodization by a historian famous as a periodizer and the other on the weaknesses of previous schemes by a historian known for his original studies of the T'ang dynasty, serve finally to suggest widespread concerns.

In a review of a book of Marxian and economic-determinist essays, Professor Miyazaki asserts the central importance of periodization but doubts that the mechanical fixing of elements in a society at any time will produce a period. Instead, a period arises as the result of a historian's evaluation and becomes established when it inspires other historians in their work. He defends objective, scientific methods in history, but in stressing the importance of evaluation and the fruitfulness of periodization among scholars of the time, he seems to speak for the view that history acquires its meanings in the minds of historians.

Professor E. G. Pulleyblank, without commenting on the idea of periodization itself, asserts that theoretical historians have in general applied preconceived notions to China, to the detriment of an understanding of Chinese history in terms of its own evidence. He acknowledges the value of hypotheses and analogies. When used with conscious reserve they may stimulate understanding without imposing a common pattern on all histories. He proposes, however, that the most satisfactory investigation of world history will come from the discovery of direct influences of one society on others. From one man, proponent of a theory, and another, sceptical of theories proposed, arises a common feeling that much remains to be said.

[NOTE: Footnotes have generally been omitted from the selections that follow, except where needed to explain the text.]

CHRONOLOGY

B.C.
(Dates before 722 are traditional)

2205   Hsia dynasty founded

1766   Shang (Yin) dynasty founded

1122–221   Chou dynasty
         722–481   Spring and Autumn period
         551–c. 233   Period of the classical philosophers
         403–221   Warring States period

221–207   Ch'in dynasty

202–A.D. 9   Former Han dynasty

A.D.

9–23   Reign of Wang Mang

25–220   Latter Han dynasty

222–589   Period of the Six Dynasties
         220–280   Period of the Three Kingdoms — Wei, Shu, Wu
         280–420   Chin dynasty
         ca. 301–*ca.* 439   Period of the Five Barbarians and Sixteen Kingdoms
         ca. 317–589   Period of the Northern and Southern Dynasties

589–618   Sui dynasty

618–906   T'ang dynasty
         755   An Lu-shan rebellion

907–960   Period of the Five Dynasties

947–1125   Liao (Khitan) dynasty

960–1279   Sung dynasty
         960–1127   Northern Sung
         1127–1279   Southern Sung

1115–1234   Chin (Jurchen) dynasty

1260–1368   Yüan (Mongol) dynasty

1368–1644   Ming dynasty

1644–1911   Ch'ing (Manchu) dynasty
         1839–1842   Anglo-Chinese (Opium) War
         1850–1864   Taiping Rebellion

1912   Republic founded
         1926   Beginning of Northern Expedition of Kuomintang

1949   People's Republic founded

The Conflict of Opinion

". . . The way of the Three Dynasties of old is like a cycle which, when it ends, must begin over again."

— Ssu-ma Ch'ien

"It has always been my observation that periods of order or disorder, of the rise and fall of different dynasties, are not interrelated. . . . Each period has its own history, and it is sufficient to cover in full the period from the beginning to the end of the dynasty without referring to other dynasties or attempting to draw parallels. Laws and institutions, however, are actually interrelated. . . . But there is no work which deals with institutions which depend for their understanding upon historical continuity."

— Ma Tuan-lin

"With the Empire of China History has to begin, for it is the oldest, as far as history gives us any information; and its *principle* has such substantiality, that for the empire in question it is at once the oldest and the newest. Early do we see China advancing to the condition in which it is found at this day; for as the contrast between objective existence and subjective freedom of movement in it, is still wanting, every change is excluded, and the fixedness of a character which recurs perpetually, takes the place of what we should call the truly historical. China and India lie, as it were, still outside the World's History, as the mere presupposition of elements whose combination must be waited for to constitute their vital progress."

— G. W. F. Hegel

"If we turn to the history of the main body of the Far Eastern Society in China, in which the moment of breakdown may be equated with the break-up of the T'ang empire in the last quarter of the ninth century of the Christian Era, we can trace the subsequent process of disintegration following its normal course through a 'time of troubles' into a universal state, only to be pulled up in the course of this stage by a reaction of the same abrupt and passionate kind as the Egyptiac reaction to the Hyksos invaders. . . . And there has been a corresponding similarity in the sequel. For the Far Eastern Society has prolonged its existence in a petrified form instead of passing expeditiously through disintegration into dissolution by way of a universal state running out into an interregnum."

— Arnold J. Toynbee

"It must be admitted . . . that there is considerable validity to the Chinese concept of the dynastic cycle, if one interprets it as a somewhat superficial political pattern that overlay the more fundamental technological, economic, social, and cultural developments."

— Edwin O. Reischauer

"Chinese civilization may be said to have undergone two cycles. The first cycle, from the dim beginnings to 383 A.D., is that of Classical China, during which the race remained comparatively pure and its culture indigenous, with only slight and insignificant cultural infiltrations from without. The second cycle, from 383 A.D. to the present, is that of Tartar-Buddhist China, . . . characterized by repeated conquests of the country by peoples from the north and by the gradual transformation of the classical civilization by Buddhism into a new synthesis, which, though still essentially Chinese, exhibits a rather thick veneer of the alien culture."

— H. T. Lei

"Now, with reference to the methods of study of European history, we would propose for consideration a periodization of East Asian history divided into four ages: Age I, the establishment of an ancient empire; Age II, an aristocratic society; Age III, a period of autocratic government; and Age IV, a period of modernizing progress in East Asia."

— Miyazaki Ichisada

"In the field of study of the history of the Chinese ancient period, China's historians affirm that the various forms and individual historical stages in the development of society as experienced by mankind have been experienced in the same way in China. In China have been experienced the primitive communal system, slave system, and feudal system; and, moreover, before the capitalism of foreign countries invaded China, even spontaneously generated buds of the elements of capitalism were in the mercantile economy of the feudal society of China."

— Chien Po-tsan

"Thus after a primitive (tribal) hydraulic beginning China moved very slowly from a 'simple' hydraulic society (with a regulated land system and little private handicraft and commerce) to a 'semi-complex' hydraulic society (which still had a regulated land system, but increased private handicraft and trade) and then quickly to a 'complex' hydraulic society with a considerable development of both mobile and immobile private property. Except for a temporary regression to a regulated land system, which lasted from the fifth to the eighth century A.D., China perpetuated itself as a complex hydraulic society throughout the imperial period, that is, roughly speaking, for almost two thousand years."

— Karl A. Wittfogel

I. EARLY CHINESE VIEWS

From the *Book of Rites*

This passage from the *Book of Rites* (*Li chi*) is one of the most celebrated in Confucian literature. It has been traditionally taken as representing Confucius' highest ideal in the social order, the age of Grand Unity (*ta-t'ung*), in which the world was shared by all the people (*t'ien-hsia wei kung*). . . . Following the age of Grand Unity came the rise of dynastic rule, [according to tradition, from 2205 B.C.].

The *Book of Rites* is a collection of essays compiled during the Han dynasty [202 B.C.–220 A.D.] from earlier writings. The present text is the opening portion of an essay on the "Evolution of Rites" (*Li-yün*), a subject which assumed the greatest importance in the Han dynasty. Moreover there are strong evidences in this piece of the syncretic tendencies of the Han, which suggest that the primitive ideal of Grand Harmony is actually a Taoist conception, while the age of Lesser Prosperity following it is the original sage-king ideal of Confucius and Mencius downgraded one step. Thus we are surprised to learn that the adoption in this period of typically Confucian institutions and ethics results in the prevalence of intrigue and war. Yet what appealed to the Chinese mind in this scheme was its apparent reconciliation of the primitive ideal and the historical actuality as two aspects of a common process. [Note that the causes of the shift from one aspect to the other are not given.]

ONCE Confucius was taking part in the winter sacrifice. After the ceremony was over, he went for a stroll along the top of the city gate and sighed mournfully. He sighed for the state of Lu.

His disciple Yen Yen [Tzu Lu], who was by his side, asked: "Why should the gentleman sigh?"

Confucius replied:

The practice of the Great Way, the illustrious men of Three Dynasties — these I shall never know in person. And yet they inspire my ambition! When the Great Way was practiced, the world was shared by all alike. The worthy and the able were promoted to office and men practiced good faith and lived in affection. Therefore they did not regard as parents only their own parents, or as sons only their own sons. The aged found a fitting close to their lives, the robust their proper employment; the young were provided with an upbringing and the widow and widower, the orphaned and the sick, with proper care. Men had their tasks and women their hearths. They hated to see goods lying about in waste, yet they did not hoard them for themselves; they disliked the thought that their energies were not fully used, yet they used them not for private ends. Therefore all evil plotting was prevented and thieves and rebels did not arise, so that people could leave their outer gates unbolted. This was the age of Grand Unity.

Now the Great Way has become hid and the world is the possession of private families. Each regards as parents only his own parents, as sons only his own sons; goods and labor are employed for selfish ends. Hereditary offices and titles are granted by ritual law while walls and moats must provide security. Ritual

From Wm. Theodore de Bary, Burton Watson, and Wing-tsit Chan, eds., *Sources of Chinese Tradition* (New York, 1960), pp. 191–192, including headnote. Reprinted by permission of Columbia University Press.

and righteousness are used to regulate the relationship between ruler and subject, to insure affection between father and son, peace between brothers, and harmony between husband and wife, to set up social institutions, organize the farms and villages, honor the brave and wise, and bring merit to the individual. Therefore intrigue and plotting come about and men take up arms. Emperor Yü, kings T'ang, Wen, Wu, and Ch'eng and the Duke of Chou achieved eminence for this

reason: that all six rulers were constantly attentive to ritual, made manifest their righteousness and acted in complete faith. They exposed error, made humanity their law and humility their practice, showing the people wherein they should constantly abide. If there were any who did not abide by these principles, they were dismissed from their positions and regarded by the multitude as dangerous. This is the period of Lesser Prosperity.

The Cyclical Succession of Dynasties

SSU-MA CH'IEN

During the Han dynasty (202 B.C.–220 A.D.), a theory of a cyclical process in all events in nature (and the world altogether) became influential in Chinese thinking. Beginning with the elemental forces of nature — the Five Agents — and extending to colors, directions, animals, planets, and other things, mutual correspondences and sequences came to be used in explanation of events, even of the succession of dynasties and dominant virtues that came to be associated with them. An abridged chart of one arrangement of correspondences (not necessarily the same as those expressed in the selection below; different authors speak of somewhat different arrangements) might look like this:

AGENT	Fire	Earth	Metal	Water	Wood
VIRTUE	Wisdom	Faith	Right-eousness	Decorum	Benevo-lence
COLOR	Red	Yellow	White	Black	Green
DYNASTY or RULER	Emp. Yao	Emp. Shun	Emp. Yü; Hsia dyn.	Shang dyn.	Chou dyn.

Ssu-ma Ch'ien (145 B.C.?–90?), the greatest early historian of China, describes below a cycle of dynasties associated with a three-phase, rather than the usual five-phase, cycle of virtues. The idea of a five-phase cycle appears elsewhere in his work, connected with correspondences between the Five Agents, colors, and animals.

THE Grand Historian remarks: The government of the Hsia dynasty was marked by good faith, which in time deteriorated until mean men had turned it into rusticity. Therefore the men of Shang

who succeeded to the Hsia reformed this defect through the virtue of piety. But piety degenerated until mean men had made it a superstitious concern for the spirits. Therefore the men of Chou who

From Burton Watson, *Records of the Grand Historian of China Translated from the* Shih chi *of Ssu-ma Ch'ien* (New York, 1961), Vol. I, pp. 118, 119. Reprinted by permission of Columbia University Press.

followed corrected this fault through refinement and order. But refinement again deteriorated until it became in the hands of the mean a mere hollow show. Therefore what was needed to reform this hollow show was a return to good faith, for the way of the Three Dynasties of old is like a cycle which, when it ends, must begin over again.

It is obvious that in late Chou and Ch'in times the earlier refinement and order had deteriorated. But the government of Ch'in failed to correct this fault, instead adding its own harsh punishments and laws. Was this not a grave error?

Thus when the Han rose to power it took over the faults of its predecessors and worked to change and reform them, causing men to be unflagging in their efforts and following the order properly ordained by Heaven. It held its court in the tenth month,[1] and its vestments and carriage tops were yellow, with plumes on the left sides of the carriages.

[1] I.e., this was the time each year when the feudal lords were required to attend the court in person and pay their respects for the new year, which in the early Han began in this month.

Comment on Early Chinese Views

ARTHUR F. WRIGHT

While in large perspective dynasty succeeded dynasty in the order prescribed by the natural forces of the universe, at closer view each dynasty in turn passed through certain points or experiences on the curve of the cycle. The idea that all major dynasties witnessed similar experiences or phases became widespread, at least in later traditional times, and the foundation for what has been called the "dynastic cycle" recently. The following description of the traditional understanding of the dynastic cycle is by Arthur F. Wright, Professor of History at Yale University.

ONE of the most important of the regularity generalizations in traditional historiography is the dynastic cycle. On the surface this is a life-cycle analogy: polities, like men, have their periods of birth, growth, maturity, senescence, and death. Yet these successive phases were never seen as the product of natural law or blind fate. The dynamic behind them was moral, and the lessons to be drawn from the study of dynastic rise and fall were moral lessons. In its genesis a dynasty received the mandate to rule from Heaven, which recognized the justice and promise of the new regime. And at its end a dynasty lost the mandate when its performance had flouted the moral norms and destroyed the moral basis of a good society.

. . . Historians reflected long and hard on the causes of dynastic prosperity and failure. Ssu-ma Kuang (1019–86), memorializing the throne in regard to his great comprehensive history of China, said:

Disregarding my inadequacy I have constantly wished to write a chronological history . . .

From Arthur F. Wright, "On the Uses of Generalization in the Study of Chinese History," in Louis Gottschalk, ed. *Generalization in the Writing of History* (Chicago, 1963), pp. 41–43. Copyright 1963 by The University of Chicago. All rights reserved. Published 1963.

taking in all that a prince ought to know — everything pertaining to the rise and fall of dynasties and the good and ill fortune of the common people, all good and bad examples that can furnish models and warning.

The great historian views the rise and fall of dynasties as an established rhythm, but he implies that a wise prince can learn from past cycles to make the moral choices that will protract the prosperity of his house.

The notion of the dynastic cycle gave rise in turn to a host of related regularity generalizations. For example, it was often argued that the phase of prosperity was correlated with the length of individual reigns, that the influence of women at court was both a symptom and a cause of dynastic decline, that "when officials are oppressive, the people rebel" — a syndrome of decline. The "bad-last ruler" of a dynasty became a stock figure who played out his role in a recurrent pattern of amoral behavior — thus demonstrating the justness of Heaven in conferring the mandate on the challenger, the "good" founder of a new dynasty.

The dynastic cycle and its related regularity generalizations were not hypotheses for the detached interpretation of historical events. Rather they comprised a symptomatology of political life which provided rulers and statesmen with material for political diagnosis and prescription. Moreover, when the symptomatology became the basis of behavior for those in power, their actions tended to sustain the regularity. For example, when Chinese statesmen thought they discerned the classic symptoms of dynastic decline, they began to qualify the support they gave to the ruling house and thus contributed to its ultimate collapse.

"Dynastic cycle" implies for the Westerner sequences of political events, but the persistent holism that was part of the self-image of Chinese civilization meant that the phases of the cycle were thought to be reflected in all areas of culture — creativity in poetry and painting, the ethos of the peasant villages, the morals and mores of the elite, the tone and tenor of popular songs and drama, the rise and fall of the price level. It is not surprising, therefore, to find regularity generalizations that correlate effete or overornamented literary styles with dynastic decline. Vapid philosophizing ("empty words"), obscene or subversive popular songs, moral slackness, and greed among the elite were similarly correlated.

In the major regularity generalization that is the dynastic cycle and in all its corollaries we see the formative influence of the self-image, notably the holistic ideal, the belief in moral dynamics and a pronounced Sinocentrism; as Professor Liensheng Yang points out, traditional discussions of the cycle focused on factors at work in the "Central Kingdom" and ignored or underrated alien influences.

Proponents of Continual History

LÜ TSU-CH'IEN, CHENG CH'IAO, MA TUAN-LIN, HUANG TSUNG-HSI, AND KU YEN-WU

Although not all the scholars represented in the following brief selections directly attack the dividing of history by dynasties, the first three, men of the Sung and Yüan dynasties (960–1279, 1279–1368), emphasize the value of seeing history as continual in some aspects, and the third of them points explicitly to the interrelationship of laws and institutions between one dynasty and the next. Lü Tsu-ch'ien (1137–1181), historian and classical scholar, asserts the need to think of history as a process of change, not as a sequence of periods, and to know how to select from among the many facts available those that elucidate change. Cheng Ch'iao (1108–1166), in the "General Preface" to his history of the entire past of China, the T'ung chih, sees history as a continuous stream of "meeting and joining" and the one-dynasty view as a hindrance to the sense of continuity. Ma Tuan-lin (thirteenth century), writer of the Wen-hsien t'ung k'ao, a great work on institutional history, further questions the regularity of a dynastic pattern and the validity of the dynastic period for the study of laws and institutions. He agrees that a dynasty's political history may be discussed without attention to other dynasties. He asserts, however, that dynasties do not follow parallel courses of political fortune, calling into question the naturalistic, cyclical view, and points out that laws and institutions carry on across dynasties.

The last two men suggest the outlines of a periodization along similar lines, though neither is writing history proper. Huang Tsung-hsi (1610–1695), a scholar in many fields, including intellectual history and political and economic criticism, was interested in explaining through history the failure of a native Chinese dynasty, the Ming, before the Manchu conquerors from the north. Here he notes a great difference between the "law" (political and social systems) of the ancient Three Dynasties and the systems of the self-seeking dynasties that followed, suggesting in effect a periodization according to institutions. In seeing two major upheavals, or turning points, in the Ch'in and Mongol Yüan dynasties, he implies a view of periods that override changes of individual dynasties. The last scholar, Ku Yen-wu (1613–1682), was a major historian who sought like Huang to understand the weaknesses of the systems of the past. In the selection he, too, exemplifies an attention to institutions that transcend dynasties when he explains the well-being of the state in terms of feudal and prefectural systems. His suggestion of combining the "meaning" of feudalism, by which he apparently means the responsible and humane attitude of government that follows from granting local officials their proper dignity, with the prefectural system to bring a new order implies a state of affairs that would constitute a new period, not a repetition of past cycles.

It is noteworthy that both Huang and Ku, viewing history through institutions, agree on the Ch'in-Han era as a great turning point, a view held also, sometimes without the older expressions of moral disapproval, in several modern schemes of periodization. The comments of both men indicate the possibility within the Chinese tradition of an approach different from that of the dynastic pattern.

A Discussion of History

LÜ TSU-CH'IEN

Ch'en Ying-chung [Ch'en Kuan] once remarked that the *General Mirror* is like Medicine Mountain: anywhere you pick you always are sure of getting something. But though it may be Medicine Mountain, you must know how to select, for if you do not know how to select, you will end up with nothing more than a vast collection of facts crammed into your memory. Hu Ch'iu Tzu once asked Lieh Tzu why he liked to travel. Lieh Tzu replied: "Other men travel in order to see what there is to see, but I travel in order to observe how things change." This might be taken as a rule for observing history. Most people, when they examine history, simply look at periods of order and realize that they are ordered, periods of disorder and recognize their disorder, observe one fact and know no more than that one fact. But is this real observation of history? You should picture yourself actually in the situation, observe which things are profitable and which dangerous, and note the misfortunes and ills of the times. Shut the book and think for yourself. Imagine that you are facing these various facts and then decide what you think ought to be done. If you look at history in this way, then your learning will increase and your intelligence improve. Then you will get real profit from your reading.

General Preface to the T'ung Chih

CHENG CH'IAO

The many rivers run each a separate course, but all must meet in the sea; only thus may the land be spared the evil of inundation. The myriad states have each their different ways, but all must join in the greater community which is China; only then may the outlying areas escape the ills of stagnation. Great is this principle of meeting and joining! From the time when books were first invented, there have been many who set forth their words, but only "Confucius was a sage endowed by Heaven unlimitedly." Therefore he brought together the *Odes* and *History*, the *Rites* and music, and joined them by his own hand so that all the literature of the world met in him. From the deeds of the two emperors Yao and Shun and the kings of the Three Dynasties he created one school of philosophy so that men of later times could fully comprehend the evolutions of past and present. Thus was his way brilliant and enlightened, surpassing all the ages before and all the ages after him.

After Confucius passed away, the various philosophers of the hundred schools appeared and in imitation of the *Analects* each composed a book setting forth his

From de Bary, Watson, and Chan, *Sources of Chinese Tradition*, pp. 496–501, 590–593, 611–612. Reprinted by permission.

general principles. But no one undertook to carry on the record of the historical facts of ensuing ages. Then in the Han, around the year 140 and later, Ssu-ma T'an and his son Ssu-ma Ch'ien appeared. The Ssu-ma family had for generations been in charge of documents and records and they were skilled at compilation and writing. Therefore they were able to understand the intention of Confucius, to join together the narratives of the *Odes* and *History*, the *Tso Commentary*, the *Narratives of the States*, the *Genealogical Origins*, the *Intrigues of the Warring States*, and the *Spring and Autumn of Ch'u and Han*, to cover the ages from the Yellow Emperor and Yao and Shun down to the Ch'in and Han, and complete one book. It was divided into five sections: the basic annals, which are recorded year by year, the hereditary houses covering the states that were handed down from generation to generation, the chronological tables which corrected dates, the treatises which dealt with specific subjects, and the memoirs devoted to the lives of individuals. For a hundred generations the official historians have not been able to depart from this model, nor have scholars ever succeeded in seriously challenging this work. After the Six Classics, there is only this one book. . . .

Confucius took the *Spring and Autumn*

form and employed it first and the scholar Tso followed this example, so that their works stand today like the sun and the moon. . . . But since the *Spring and Autumn Annals,* only the *Shih chi* has succeeded in making use of this model of composition. Unfortunately Pan Ku was not the man he should have been, and he failed to grasp the principle of joining and penetrating, and from his time the followers of the Ssu-ma family fell away. . . . Later historians have lost no time in running after the example of Pan Ku, seemingly unable to judge the relative merits of his work and that of Ssu-ma Ch'ien. But Ssu-ma Ch'ien is to Pan Ku as a dragon is to a pig. Why then do all later historians ignore Ssu-ma Ch'ien and follow Pan Ku? . . .

Confucius said: "The Yin dynasty followed the rites of the Hsia; wherein it took from or added to them may be known. The Chou followed the rites of the Yin; wherein it took from or added to them may be known." This is what is known as the continuity of history. But from the time when Pan Ku wrote the history of only one dynasty, this principle of continuity has been ignored. Thus although one be a sage like Confucius he can never know what was taken away or what added in each period. The way of joining and meeting was from this time lost.

Preface to the General Study of Literary Remains

MA TUAN-LIN

THE philosopher Hsün Tzu long ago remarked: "If you would observe the ways of the ancient sage-kings, they are perfectly obvious, for they are the ways of the later kings. The gentleman studies the ways of these later kings and speaks of the hundred kings of long ago as easily as

another folds his hands and begins a discussion." Therefore if one studies institutions, examines laws and statutes, is widely learned and of stout understanding, then truly may he comprehend the affairs of Confucianism.

After the time of the *Odes,* the *History,*

and the *Spring and Autumn Annals,* only Ssu-ma Ch'ien deserves to be called a "good historian." He used the annal and memoir, treatise and chronological table form, the annals and memoirs to describe the periods of order and disorder, of rise and fall of states, and the eight treatises to relate matters of law and institutions. Of all the men who have since taken up brush and writing tablet, none has been able to depart from this form. But from the time of Pan Ku and thereafter, histories were written covering only one dynasty so that, much to the distress of the readers, the principle of continuity and development was lost. Finally, however, Ssu-ma Kuang wrote his *General Mirror,* covering the happenings of some 1,300 years in which he selected the narratives of seventeen separate histories and put them all together to form one work. Later scholars who have perused his pages have found all things of past and present therein. But although Ssu-ma Kuang is very detailed on matters of order and disorder, and the rise and fall of dynasties, his treatment of laws and institutions is very sketchy. This is not because of any lack of wisdom on his part, but simply that, his material being so voluminous, he was forced to focus his narrative upon certain problems only and thus neglect others.

It has always been my observation that periods of order or disorder, of the rise and fall of different dynasties, are not interrelated. The way the Chin came to power, for example, was not the same as the way the Han came to power, while the fall of the Sui was quite different from the fall of the T'ang. Each period has its own history, and it is sufficient to cover in full the period from the beginning to the end of the dynasty without referring to other dynasties or attempting to draw parallels. Laws and institutions, however, are actually interrelated. The Yin followed the rites of the Hsia, the Chou followed those of the Yin, and whoever follows the rites of Chou, though it be a hundred generations after, the way in which he takes from or adds to them may be known. This was the prediction made by the Sage, Confucius. Thus from the Ch'in and the Han down to the T'ang and the Sung, the regulations concerning rites, music, warfare, and punishments, the system for taxation and selection of officials, even the changes and elaborations in bureaucratic titles or the developments and alternations in geography, although in the end not necessarily the same for all dynasties, yet did not suddenly spring into being as something unique for each period. Thus the court etiquette and governmental system of the Han was based upon regulations of the Ch'in; the military and tax systems of the T'ang were based upon Chou statutes. Therefore to understand the reasons for the gradual growth and relative importance of institutions in each period, you must make a comprehensive and comparative study of them from their beginnings to their ends and in this way try to grasp their development; otherwise you will encounter serious difficulties. The type of political history that is not dependent upon continuity has already been amply covered in Ssu-ma Kuang's book, but there is no work which deals with institutions which depend for their understanding upon historical continuity. Is it not fitting that scholars of our time should turn their full attention to this problem?

On Law

HUANG TSUNG-HSI

UNTIL the end of the Three Dynasties there was law. Since the Three Dynasties there has been no law. Why do I say so? Because the Two Emperors and Three Kings knew that mankind could not do without sustenance and therefore gave men fields to cultivate. They knew that men could not do without clothes and therefore gave them land on which to grow mulberry and hemp. They knew also that men could not go untaught, so they set up schools, established the marriage ceremony to guard against promiscuity, and instituted military service to guard against disorders. This constituted law[1] until the end of the Three Dynasties. It was never laid down for the benefit of one man alone.

Later rulers, once they had won the world, feared only that their dynasty might not last long and that their descendants would be unable to preserve their empire. To prevent what they feared from happening, they resorted to laws. Consequently, what they called "law" was simply instituted for the sake of one family and not for the sake of all mankind.

Thus the Ch'in abolished feudal fiefs and set up commanderies (chün) and prefectures (hsien) thinking that this system would better serve their own interests. The Han gave domains to members of the royal house, so as to have them stand guard for the dynasty throughout the empire. The Sung abolished the military commanderies because they caused the dynasty some uneasiness. Such being their laws, how could we expect to find in them the

slightest trace of consideration for the general welfare? Indeed, could we call them "law" at all?

The law of the Three Dynasties safeguarded the world for the people. The prince did not monopolize all the wealth of the land nor did he jealously keep the right to punish and reward out of the people's hands. Position at court was not particularly considered an honor; to live an obscure life in the country was not particularly a disgrace. Later this kind of law was criticized for its looseness, but at that time the people were not envious of those in high place, nor did they despise humble status. The looser the law was, the fewer the disturbances which arose. It was what we might call "law without laws." The laws of later times safeguard the world as if it were something in the [prince's] treasure chest. It is not desired that anything beneficial should be left to the lowly, but rather that all blessings be reserved for the one on high. If the prince employs a man, he is immediately afraid that the man will act in his own interest, and so another man is employed to keep a check on the first one. If one measure is adopted, there are immediate fears of its being abused or evaded, and so another measure must be adopted to guard against abuses or evasions. All men know where the treasure chest lies, and the prince is constantly fretting and fidgeting out of anxiety for the security of the treasure. Consequently, the laws have to be made more comprehensive and detailed, and as they become more detailed, they become the very source of disorder. These are what we might call "unlawful laws."

Some say that each dynasty has its own laws and that succeeding generations of

[1] The Chinese term fa means "system" as well as legal regulation, and is applied here to the political and social institutions of ancient times, which for Huang represented a kind of basic constitution.

9

the royal house have a filial duty to follow the ancestral laws. Now the "unlawful laws" were originally instituted because the first prince of a line was unable to curb his own selfishness. Later princes, out of the same inability to curb their own selfishness, may in some cases have broken down these laws. The breaking down of the laws was admittedly a cause for suffering among the people, yet this does not mean that the original enactment of the laws never caused the people to suffer. And still some insist that we get involved in this kind of legalistic muck just to gain a little reputation for upholding the dynastic laws — all of which talk is just the secondhand drivel of petty literocrats.

It might be argued that order and disorder in the world are unrelated to the maintenance or absence of law. Now as to this there has been a great change from the past to the present: one complete upheaval which came with the Ch'in dynasty, and another with the Yüan [Mongol] dynasty. Following these two upheavals nothing at all survived of the sympathetic, benevolent, and constructive government of the early kings. So, unless we take a long-range view and look deep into the heart of the matter, changing everything thoroughly until the original order is restored with its land system, feudal system, school and military system, then even though some minor changes are made there will never be an end to the misery of the common man.

If it should be said that there are only men who govern well, not laws which govern well, my reply is that only if there are laws which govern well, will there later be men who govern well. Since "unlawful laws" fetter men hand and foot, even a man capable of governing well cannot overcome the handicaps of senseless restraint and suspicion. When there is something to be done, he does no more than his share, and since he contents himself with trifling accomplishments, there can be no outstanding achievements. If the law of the early kings were restored, there would be a spirit among men which went beyond the letter of the law. If men were of the right kind, the full intent of the law would be fulfilled; and even if they were of the wrong kind, it would be impossible for them to govern tyrannically and make the people suffer. Therefore I say we must first have laws which govern well and later we shall have men who govern well.

The Feudal System vs. the Prefectural System

KU YEN-WU

IF we understand why the feudal system changed into the prefectural system, we will also understand that as the prefectural system in turn falls into decay it too must change. Does this mean that there will be a return to feudalism? No, this is impossible. But if some sage were to appear who could invest the prefectural system with the essential meaning of feudalism, then the world would attain order.

. . . Today the prefectural system has reached a point of extreme decay, but no such sage appears and people go on doing everything in the same old way. Therefore with each day the people become poorer, China grows weaker, and we hasten down the road to ruin. Why is this? The fault of feudalism was its concentration of power on the local level, while the fault of the prefectural system is its concentration of power at the top. The sage-rulers of antiquity were impartial and public-minded in their treatment of all men, parceling out land to them and dividing up their domains. But now the ruler considers all the territory within the four seas to be his own prefecture, and is still unsatisfied. He suspects every person, he handles every affair that comes up, so that each day the directives and official documents pile higher than the day before. On top of this he sets up supervisors, provincial governors and governors-general, supposing that in this way he can keep the local officials from tyrannizing over and harming the people. He is unaware that these officials in charge are concerned only in moving with utmost caution so as to stay out of trouble until they have the good fortune to be relieved of their posts, and are quite unwilling to undertake anything of profit to the people. Under such circumstances how can the people avoid poverty and the nation escape debilitation? If this situation is allowed to continue unchanged, I am positive that it will lead only to chaos with trouble increasing day by day. If, however, the position of local officials is accorded its proper dignity, and such officials are granted fiscal and administrative authority, if the post of supervisor is discontinued, the enticement of hereditary office held out to officials, and a method whereby they may select their own subordinates put into effect, this will achieve the goal of imbuing the prefectural system with the essential meaning of feudalism, and the decay that has come about in the last two thousand years can be remedied. Rulers hereafter will find that if they hope to improve the livelihood of the people and strengthen the power of the nation, they must heed my words.

II. WORLD HISTORY FROM THE WEST

The Childhood of History

G. W. F. HEGEL

Georg Wilhelm Friedrich Hegel (1770–1831), by reason of his great intellectual authority, represents strongly certain European ideas about history and China's experience. One of the best-known of his many influential concepts — that of the dialectical progress — is not illustrated here; but the selections contain others repeated or reflected in later theories about China, the ideas of the Oriental despot as possessor of all power, Chinese history as a repetitive circle without advance, and Chinese society as one of absolute equality without freedom. Of even more general significance in the modern attempts at periodization is the lineal view of history.

I T is only an inference from the history of the World, that its development has been a rational process; that the history in question has constituted the rational necessary course of the World-Spirit — that Spirit whose nature is always one and the same, but which unfolds this its one nature in the phenomena of the World's existence. This must, as before stated, present itself as the ultimate *result* of History.

*   *   *

The inquiry into the *essential destiny* of Reason — as far as it is considered in reference to the World — is identical with the question, *What is the ultimate design of the World?* And the expression implies that that design is destined to be realized. Two points of consideration suggest themselves; first, the *import* of this design — its abstract definition; and secondly, its *realization*.

It must be observed at the outset, that the phenomenon we investigate — Universal History — belongs to the realm of *Spirit*.

*   *   *

The nature of Spirit may be understood by a glance at its direct opposite — *Matter*. As the essence of Matter is Gravity, so, on the other hand, we may affirm that the substance, the essence of Spirit is Freedom. All will readily assent to the doctrine that Spirit, among other properties, is also endowed with Freedom; but philosophy teaches that all the qualities of Spirit exist only through Freedom; that all are but means for attaining Freedom; that all seek and produce this and this alone. It is a result of speculative Philosophy, that Freedom is the sole truth of Spirit. Matter possesses gravity in virtue of its tendency toward a central point. It is essentially composite; consisting of parts that *exclude* each other. It seeks its Unity; and therefore exhibits itself as self-destructive, as verging toward its opposite [an indivisible point]. If it could attain this, it would be Matter

From G. W. F. Hegel, *Philosophy of History*, rev. ed., tr. J. Sibree (New York, Collier, 1905), selections from the Introduction, "The Classification of Historical Data," and Part I: "The Oriental World."

no longer, it would have perished. It strives after the realization of its Idea; for in Unity it exists *ideally*. Spirit, on the contrary, may be defined as that which has its center in itself. It has not a unity outside itself, but has already found it; it exists *in* and *with itself*. Matter has its essence out of itself; Spirit is *self-contained existence* (Bei-sich-selbst-seyn). Now this is Freedom, exactly. For if I am dependent, my being is referred to something else which I am not; I cannot exist independently of something external. I am free, on the contrary, when my existence depends upon myself. This self-contained existence of Spirit is none other than self-consciousness — consciousness of one's own being. Two things must be distinguished in consciousness; first, the fact *that I know*; secondly, *what I know*. In *self*-consciousness these are merged in one; for Spirit *knows itself*. It involves an appreciation of its own nature, as also an energy enabling it to realize itself; to make itself *actually* that which it is *potentially*. According to this abstract definition it may be said of Universal History, that it is the exhibition of Spirit in the process of working out the knowledge of that which it is potentially. And as the germ bears in itself the whole nature of the tree, and the taste and form of its fruits, so do the first traces of Spirit virtually contain the whole of that History. The Orientals have not attained the knowledge that Spirit — Man *as such* — is free; and because they do not know this, they are not free. They only know that *one is free*. But on this very account, the freedom of that one is only caprice; ferocity — brutal recklessness of passion, or a mildness and tameness of the desires, which is itself only an accident of Nature — mere caprice like the former. That *one* is therefore only a Despot; not a *free man*. The consciousness of Freedom first arose among the Greeks, and therefore they were free; but they, and the Romans likewise, knew only that *some* are free — not man as such. Even Plato and Aristotle did not know this. The Greeks, therefore, had slaves; and

their whole life and the maintenance of their splendid liberty, was implicated with the institution of slavery: a fact moreover, which made that liberty on the one hand only an accidental, transient and limited growth; on the other hand, constituted it a rigorous thraldom of our common nature — of the Human. The German nations, under the influence of Christianity, were the first to attain the consciousness, that man, as man, is free: that it is the *freedom* of Spirit which constitutes its essence.

*   *   *

The general statement given above, of the various grades in the consciousness of Freedom — and which we applied in the first instance to the fact that the Eastern nations knew only that *one* is free; the Greek and Roman world only that *some* are free; while *we* know that all men absolutely (man *as man*) are free — supplies us with the natural division of Universal History, and suggests the mode of its discussion.

*   *   *

The History of the World travels from East to West, for Europe is absolutely the end of History, Asia the beginning. The History of the World has an East κατ' ἐξοχήν; (the term East in itself is entirely relative), for although the Earth forms a sphere, History performs no circle round it, but has on the contrary a determinate East, viz., Asia. . . . The East knew and to the present day knows only that *One* is Free; the Greek and Roman world, that *some* are free; the German World knows that *All* are free. The first political form therefore which we observe in History, is *Despotism*, the second *Democracy* and *Aristocracy*, the third *Monarchy*.

*   *   *

The first phase — that with which we have to begin — is the *East*. Unreflected consciousness — substantial, objective, spiritual existence — forms the basis; to which the subjective will first sustains a relation in the form of faith, confidence, obedience. In the political life of the East we find a realized rational freedom, developing itself without advancing to *subjective* freedom. It is the childhood of History. Substantial forms constitute the gorgeous edifices of Oriental *Empires* in which we find all rational ordinances and arrangements, but in such a way, that individuals remain as mere accidents. These revolve round a center, round the sovereign, who, as patriarch — not as despot in the sense of the *Roman* Imperial Constitution — stands at the head. For he has to enforce the moral and substantial: he has to uphold those essential ordinances which are already established; so that what among us belongs entirely to subjective freedom, here proceeds from the entire and general body of the State. The glory of Oriental conception is the One Individual as that substantial being to which all belongs, so that no other individual has a separate existence, or mirrors himself in his subjective freedom. All the riches of imagination and Nature are appropriated to that dominant existence in which subjective freedom is essentially merged; the latter looks for its dignity *not* in itself, but in that absolute object. All the elements of a complete State — even subjectivity — may be found there, but not yet harmonized with the grand substantial being. For outside the One Power — before which nothing can maintain an independent existence — there is only revolting caprice, which, beyond the limits of the central power, roves at will without purpose or result. Accordingly we find the wild hordes breaking out from the Upland — falling upon the countries in question, and laying them waste, or settling down in them, and giving up their wild life; but in all cases resultlessly lost in the central substance. This phase of Substantiality, since it has not taken up its antithesis into itself and overcome it, directly divides itself into two elements. On the one side we see duration, stability — Empires belonging to mere space, as it were [as distinguished from Time] — unhistorical History; — as for example, in China, the State based on the Family relation; — a paternal Government, which holds together the constitution by its provident care, its admonitions, retributive or rather disciplinary inflictions; — a prosaic Empire, because the antithesis of Form, viz., Infinity, Ideality, has not yet asserted itself. On the other side, the Form of Time stands contrasted with this spatial stability. The States in question, without undergoing any change in themselves, or in the principle of their existence, are constantly changing their position towards each other. They are in ceaseless conflict, which brings on rapid destruction. The opposing principle of individuality enters into these conflicting relations; but it is itself as yet only unconscious, merely natural Universality — Light, which is not yet the light of the personal soul. This History, too (i.e., of the struggles before-mentioned) is, for the most part, really *unhistorical*, for it is only the repetition of the same majestic ruin. The new element, which in the shape of bravery, prowess, magnanimity, occupies the place of the previous despotic pomp, goes through the same circle of decline and subsidence. This subsidence is therefore not really such, for through all this restless change no advance is made.

* * *

With the Empire of China History has to begin, for it is the oldest, as far as history gives us any information; and its *principle* has such substantiality, that for the empire in question it is at once the oldest and the newest. Early do we see China advancing to the condition in which it is found at this day; for as the contrast between objective existence and subjective freedom of movement in it, is still wanting, every change is excluded, and the fixedness of a character which recurs perpetually, takes the place of what we should call the truly historical. China and India lie, as it were, still outside the World's History, as the mere presupposition of elements whose combination must be waited for to constitute their vital progress. . . .

A Morphology of World History

OSWALD SPENGLER

The idea of a cycle in history, never a Chinese monopoly, led in the world history of Oswald Spengler (1880–1936) to a picture of a world field in which flower after flower of culture came to bloom and died. In contrast to the traditional Chinese theory, culture could grow in many different societies and, in a manner somewhat reminiscent of that pictured by Hegel, would harden in death as a fossil, or "civilization," the condition of China since the first century of the Christian era. History being a repetition of the same process in culture after culture, Spengler holds that it is possible, by drawing correct "morphological" analogies, to show the "contemporary" epochs of all major cultures.

CULTURES are organisms, and world-history is their collective biography. Morphologically, the immense history of the Chinese or of the Classical Culture is the exact equivalent of the petty history of the individual man, or of the animal, or the tree, or the flower. . . . If we want to learn to recognize inward forms that constantly and everywhere repeat themselves, the comparative morphology[1] of plants and animals has long ago given us the methods. In the destinies of the several Cultures that follow upon one another, grow up with one another, touch, overshadow, and suppress one another, is compressed the whole content of human history. And if we set free their shapes, till now hidden all too deep under the surface of a trite "history of human progress," and let them march past us in the spirit, it cannot but be that we shall succeed in distinguishing, amidst all that is special or unessential, the primitive culture-form, *the* Culture that underlies as ideal all the individual Cultures.

I distinguish the *idea* of a Culture, which is the sum total of its inner possibilities, from its sensible *phenomenon* or appearance upon the canvas of history as a fulfilled actuality. It is the relation of the soul to the living body, to its expression in the light-world perceptible to our eyes. This history of a Culture is the progressive actualizing of its possible, and the fulfilment is equivalent to the end.

*   *   *

Culture is the *prime phenomenon* of all past and future world-history. The deep, and scarcely appreciated, idea of Goethe, which he discovered in his "living nature" and always made the basis of his morphological researches, we shall here apply — in its most precise sense — to all the formations of man's history, whether fully matured, cut off in the prime, half opened or stifled in the seed. It is the method of living into (erfühlen) the object, as opposed to dissecting it.

*   *   *

A Culture is born in the moment when a great soul awakens out of the proto-spirituality (*dem urseelenhaften Zustande*)

---

[1] Not the dissecting morphology of the Darwinian's pragmatic zoology with its hunt for causal connexions, but the seeing and overseeing morphology of Goethe.

of ever-childish humanity, and detaches itself, a form from the formless, a bounded
and mortal thing from the boundless and
enduring. It blooms on the soil of an ex-
actly-definable landscape, to which plant-
wise it remains bound. It dies when this
soul has actualized the full sum of its possibilities in the shape of peoples, languages,
dogmas, arts, states, sciences, and reverts
into the proto-soul. But its living existence,
that sequence of great epochs which define
and display the stages of fulfilment, is an
inner passionate struggle to maintain the
Idea against the powers of Chaos without
and the unconscious muttering deep-down
within. It is not only the artist who struggles against the resistance of the material
and the stifling of the idea within him.
Every Culture stands in a deeply-symboli-
cal, almost in a mystical, relation to the
Extended, the space, in which and through
which it strives to actualize itself. The aim
once attained — the idea, the entire content of inner possibilities, fulfilled and
made externally actual — the Culture suddenly hardens, it mortifies, its blood con-
geals, its force breaks down, and it becomes
Civilization, the thing which we feel and
understand in the words Egypticism, By-
zantinism, Mandarinism. As such they
may, like a worn-out giant of the primeval
forest, thrust their decaying branches towards the sky for hundreds or thousands
of years, as we see in China, in India, in
the Islamic world. It was thus that the
Classical Civilization rose gigantic, in the
Imperial age, with a false semblance of
youth and strength and fullness, and
robbed the young Arabian Culture of the
East of light and air.

*   *   *

For every Culture has *its own* Civilization. In this work, for the first time the
two words, hitherto used to express an
indefinite, more or less ethical, distinction,
are used in a *periodic* sense, to express a
strict and necessary *organic succession*. The
Civilization is the inevitable *destiny* of the
Culture, and in this principle we obtain

the viewpoint from which the deepest and
gravest problems of historical morphology
become capable of solution. Civilizations
are the most external and artificial states
of which a species of developed humanity
is capable. They are a conclusion, the thing-
become succeeding the thing-becoming,
death following life, rigidity following expansion, intellectual age and the stone-
built, petrifying world-city following
mother-earth and the spiritual childhood
of Doric and Gothic. They are an end,
irrevocable, yet by inward necessity reached
again and again. . . .[2]

A glance over the group of the Cultures
discloses task after task. The nineteenth
century, in which historical research was
guided by natural science, and historical
thought by the ideas of the Baroque, has
simply brought us to a pinnacle whence
we see the new world at our feet. Shall we
ever take possession of that new world?

Even today uniform treatment of these
grand life-courses is immensely difficult,
because the more remote fields have not
been seriously worked up at all. Once more,
it is the lordly outlook of the West European — he will only notice that which approaches him from one or another antiquity
by the proper and respectful route of a
Middle Age, and that which goes its own
ways will get but little of his attention.
Thus, of the things of the Chinese and the
Indian worlds, certain kinds are now beginning to be tackled — art, religion, philosophy — but the political history is dealt
with, if at all, "chattily." It does not occur
to anyone to treat the great constitutional
problems of Chinese history — the Hohen-
staufen-destiny of the Li-Wang (842), the
first Congress of Princes (659), the struggle of principle between the imperialism
(Lien-heng) of the "Roman" state of Tsin
and the League-of-Nations idea (Ho-tsung)
between 500 and 300, the rise of the Chinese Augustus, Hwang-ti (221) — with
anything of the thoroughness that Momm-
sen devoted to the principate of Augustus.

[2] This paragraph has been transferred from Vol.
I, p. 31, in the original. [Editor's note]

India, again; however completely the Indians themselves have forgotten their state-history, we have after all more available material for Buddha's time than we have for history of the Classical ninth and eighth centuries, and yet even to-day we act as though "the" Indian had lived entirely in his philosophy, just as the Athenians (so our classicists would have us believe) spent their lives in beauty-philosophizing on the banks of the Ilissus. But even Egyptian politics receive little reflective attention. The later Egyptian historian concealed under the name "Hyksos period" the same crisis which the Chinese treat of under the name "Period of the Contending States" — here, too, is something never yet investigated. And interest in the Arabian world has reached to the frontier of the Classical tongues and no further. With what endless assiduity we have described the constitution of Diocletian, and assembled material for the entirely unimportant administrative history of the provinces of Asia Minor — because it is written in Greek. But the Sassanid state, the precedent and in every respect the model of Diocletian's, comes into the picture only occasionally, and then as Rome's *opponent* in war. What about *its own* administrative and juristic history? What is the poor sum-total of material that we have assembled for the law and economics of Egypt, India, and China in comparison with the work that has been done on Greek and Roman law. . . .

After 1500 three new Cultures begin — first, the Indian, in the upper Punjab; then, a hundred years later, the Chinese on the middle Hwang-Ho; and then, about 1100, the Classical, on the Ægean Sea. The Chinese historians speak of the three great dynasties of Hsia, Shang, and Chou in much the same way as Napoleon regarded himself as a fourth dynasty following the Merovingians, the Carolingians, and the Capetians — in reality, the third coexisted with the Culture right through its course in each case. When in 441 B.C. the titular Emperor of the Chou dynasty became a state pensioner of the "Eastern

Duke" and when in A.D. 1793 "Louis Capet" was executed, the Culture in each case passed into the Civilization. There are some bronzes of very great antiquity preserved from late Shang times, which stand towards the later art in exactly the same relation as Mycenæan to Early Classical pottery and Carolingian to Romanesque art. In the Vedic, Homeric, and Chinese springtimes, with their *Pfalzen* and *Burgen,* their knighthood and feudal rulership, can be seen the whole image of our Gothic, and the "period of the Great Protectors" (Ming-Chu, 685–691) corresponds precisely to the time of Cromwell, Wallenstein, and Richelieu and to the First Tyrannis of the Greek world.

The period 480–230 is called by the Chinese historians the "Period of the Contending States"; it culminated in a century of unbroken warfare between mass-armies with frightful social upheavals, and out of it came the "Roman" state of Tsin as founder of a Chinese Imperium. This phase Egypt experienced between 1780 and 1580, of which the last century was the "Hyksos" time. The Classical experienced it from Chæronea (338), and, at the high pitch of horror, from the Gracchi (133) to Actium (31 B.C.). And it is the destiny of the West-European-American world for the nineteenth and twentieth centuries.

During this period the centre of gravity changes — as from Attica to Latium, so from the Hwang-ho (at Ho-nan-fu) to the Yang-tse (modern province of Hu-pei). The Si-Kiang was as vague for the Chinese savants of those days as the Elbe for the Alexandrian geographer, and of the existence of India they had as yet no notion.

As on the other side of the globe there arose the principes of the Julian-Claudian house, so here in China there arose the mighty figure of Wang-Cheng, who led Tsin through the decisive struggle to sole supremacy and in 221 assumed the title of Ti (literally equivalent to "Augustus") and the Cæsar-name Hwang-ti. He founded the *Pax Serica,* as we may call it, carried out a grand social reform in the exhausted

"CONTEMPORARY" POLITICAL EPOCHS

	EGYPTIAN	CLASSICAL	CHINESE	WESTERN
Pre-Cultural Period.	PRIMITIVE FOLK. TRIBES AND THEIR CHIEFS. AS YET NO "POLITICS" AND NO "STATE"			
	Thinite Period (Menes) (3400–3000)	Mycenean Age ("Agamemnon") (1600–1100)	Shang Period (1700–1300)	Frankish Period (Charlemagne) (500–900)
Culture.	NATIONAL GROUPS OF DEFINITE STYLE AND PARTICULAR WORLD-FEELING. "NATIONS." WORKING OF AN IMMANENT STATE-IDEA			
I. EARLY PERIOD. *Organic articulation of political existence. The two prime classes (noble and priest). Feudal economics; purely agrarian values*				
1. Feudalism. Spirit of countryside and country-man. The "City" only a market or stronghold. Chivalric-religious ideals. Struggles of vassals amongst themselves and against overlord	OLD KINGDOM (2900–2400) Feudal conditions of IV Dynasty. Increasing power of feudatories and priesthoods The Pharaoh as incarnation of Ra	DORIC PERIOD (1100–650) The Homeric kingship Rise of the nobility (Ithaca, Etruria, Sparta)	EARLY CHOU PERIOD (1300–800) The central ruler (Wang) pressed hard by the feudal nobility	GOTHIC PERIOD (900–1500) Roman-German Imperial period Crusading nobility Empire and Papacy
2. Crisis and dissolution of patriarchal forms. From feudalism to aristocratic State	VI Dynasty. Break-up of the Kingdom into heritable principalities. VII and VIII Dynasties, interregnum	Aristocratic synoecism Dissolution of kinship into annual offices Oligarchy	934–904. I-Wang and the vassals 842. Interregnum	Territorial princes Renaissance towns. Lancaster and York 1254. Interregnum
II. LATE PERIOD. *Actualizing of the matured State-idea. Town versus countryside. Rise of Third Estate (Bourgeoisie). Victory of money over landed property*				
3. Fashioning of a world of States of strict form. Frondes	MIDDLE KINGDOM (2150–1800) XIth Dynasty. Overthrow of the baronage by the rulers of Thebes. Centralized bureaucracy-state	IONIC PERIOD (650–300) 6th Century. First Tyrannis. (Cleisthenes, Periander, Polycrates, the Tarquins.) The City-State.	LATE CHOU PERIOD (800–500) Period of the "Protectors" (Ming-Chu 685–591) and the congresses of princes (–460)	BAROQUE PERIOD (1500–1800) Dynastic family-power, and Fronde (Richelieu, Wallenstein, Cromwell) about 1630.
4. Climax of the State-form ("Absolutism") Unity of town and country ("State" and "Society," . . . "three estates")	XIIth Dynasty (2000–1788) Strictest centralization of power Court and finance nobility	The pure Polis (absolutism of the Demos). Agora politics Rise of the tribunate Themistocles, Pericles	Chun-Chiu period ("Spring" and "Autumn"), 590–480 Seven powers Perfection of social forms (Li)	Ancien Régime. Rococo. Court nobility of Versailles. Cabinet politics. Habsburg and Bourbon. Louis XIV. Frederick the Great

5. Break-up of the State-form (Revolution and Napoleonism). Victory of the city over the countryside (of the "people" over the privileged, of the intelligentsia over tradition, ...)	1788–1680. Revolution and military government. Decay of the realm. Small potentates, in some cases sprung from the people	4th Century. Social revolution and Second Tyrannis (Dionysius I, Jason of Pherae, Appius Claudius the Censor) *Alexander*	480. Beginning of the Chan-Kwo period 441. Fall of the Chou dynasty. Revolutions and annihilation-wars	End of XVIII Century. Revolution in America and France (Washington, Fox, Mirabeau, Robespierre) *Napoleon*

Civilization. THE BODY OF THE PEOPLE, NOW ESSENTIALLY URBAN IN CONSTITUTION, DISSOLVES INTO FORMLESS MASS. MEGALOPOLIS AND PROVINCES. THE FOURTH ESTATE ("MASSES"), INORGANIC, COSMOPOLITAN

1. Domination of Money ("Democracy"). Economic powers permeating the political forms and authorities	1680 (1788)–1580. Hyksos period. Deepest decline. Dictatures of alien generals (Chian). After 1600 definitive victory of the rulers of Thebes	300–100. Political Hellenism. From Alexander to Hannibal and Scipio royal all-power; from Cleomenes III and C. Flaminius (220) to C. Marius, radical demagogues	480–230. Period of the "Contending States". 288. The Imperial title. The imperialist statesmen of Tsin. From 289 incorporation of the last states in the Empire	1800–2000. XIXth Century. From Napoleon to the World-War. "System of the Great Powers," standing armies, constitutions. XXth-Century transition from constitutional to informal sway of individuals. Annihilation wars. ...
2. Formation of Cæsarism. Victory of force-politics over money. ... Inward decline of the nations into a formless population. ..., gradually-increasing crudity of despotism	1580–1350. XVIIIth Dynasty Thuthmosis III	100–0–100. Sulla to Domitian Caesar, Tiberius	250–0–26. House of Wang-Cheng and Western Han Dynasty 221. Augustus-title (Shi) of Emperor Hwang-Ti 140–80. Wu-ti	2000–2200
3. Maturing of the final form. Private and family policies of individual leaders. The world as spoil. Egypticism, Mandarinism, Byzantinism. ... enfeeblement even of the imperial machinery, against young peoples eager for spoil, or alien conquerors. Primitive human conditions slowly thrust up into the highly-civilized mode of living	1350–1205. XIXth Dynasty Sethos I Rameses II	100–300. Trajan to Aurelian Trajan, Septimius Severus	25–220 A.D. Eastern Han Dynasty 58–71. Ming-ti	after 2200

19

Empire, and — as promptly as Rome — began to build his *Limes,* the famous Great Wall, for which in 214 he annexed a part of Mongolia. He was the first, too, to subdue the barbarians south of the Yang-tse, in a series of large-scale campaigns followed and confirmed by military roads, castles, and colonies. But "Roman," too, was his family history — a Tacitean drama with Lui-ti (Chancellor and stepfather of the Emperor) and Li-Szu, the great statesman (the Agrippa of his day, and unifier of the Chinese script), playing parts, and one that quickly closed in Neronic horrors. Followed then the two Han dynasties (Western, 206 B.C.–23 A.D.; Eastern, 25–220 A.D.), under which the frontiers extended more and more, while in the capital eunuch-ministers, generals, and soldiery made and unmade the rulers at their pleasure. At certain rare moments, as under Wu-ti (140–86) and Ming-ti (58–76), the Chinese-Confucian, the Indian–Buddhist, and the Classical-Stoic world-forces approached one another so closely in the region of the Caspian that they might easily have come into actual touch.[3]

Chance decreed that the heavy attacks of the Huns should break themselves in vain upon the Chinese "Limes," which at each crisis found a strong emperor to defend it. The decisive repulse of the Huns took place in 124–119 under the Chinese Trajan, Wu-ti; and it was he, too, who finally incorporated Southern China in the Empire, with the object of obtaining a route into India, and built a grand embattled road to the Tarim. And so the Huns turned westward, and in due course they appear, impelling a swarm of Germanic tribes, in face of the Limes of the Roman world. This time they succeeded. The Roman Imperium collapsed, and thus two only of the three empires continued, and still continue, as desirable spoil for a suc-

cession of different powers. To-day it is the "red-haired barbarian" of the West who is playing before the highly civilized eyes of Brahman and Mandarin the rôle once played by Mogul and Manchu, playing it neither better nor worse than they, and certain like them to be superseded in due course by other actors.

* * *

. . . Primitive man has history only in the biological sense, and all prehistoric study boils down to the investigation of this sense. The increasing familiarity of men with fire, stone tools, and the mechanical laws which make weapons effective, characterizes only the development of the type and of its latent possibilities. The objects for which one tribe employed these weapons against another tribe are of no importance in this plane of history. Stone Age and Baroque are age-grades in the existence of respectively a genus and a Culture — i.e., two organisms belonging to two fundamentally different settings. And here I would protest against two assumptions that have so far vitiated all historical thought: the assertion of an ultimate aim of mankind as a whole and the denial of there being ultimate aims at all. The life *has* an aim. It is the fulfilment of that which was ordained at its conception. But the individual belongs by birth to the particular high Culture on the one hand and to the type Man on the other — there is no third unit of being for him. His destiny must lie either in the zoological or in the world-historical field. "Historical" man, as I understand the word and as all great historians have meant it to be taken, is the man of a Culture that is in full march towards self-fulfilment. Before this, after this, outside this, man is *historyless*; and the destinies of the people to which he belongs matter as little as the Earth's destiny matters when the plane of attention is the astronomical and not the geological.

From this there follows a fact of the most decisive importance, and one that has never before been established: that man

[3] For at that time imperialistic tendencies found expression even in India, in the Maurya and Sunga dynasty; these, however, could only be confused and ineffective, Indian nature being what it was.

is not only historyless before the birth of the Culture, but again becomes so as soon as a Civilization has worked itself out fully to the definitive form which betokens the end of the living development of the Culture and the exhaustion of the last potentialities of its significant existence. That which we see in the Egyptian Civilization after Seti I (1300) and in the Chinese, the Indian, the Arabian to this day is — notwithstanding all the cleverness of the religious, philosophical and, especially, political forms in which it is wrapped — just the old zoological up-and-down of the primitive age again. Whether the lords sitting in Babylon were wild war-hordes like the Kassites or refined inheritors like the Persians, when, for how long, and with what success they kept their seats, signified nothing from the standpoint of Babylon. The comfort of the population was affected by such things, naturally, but they made no difference either way to the fact that the soul of this world was extinct and its events, therefore, void of any deep meaning. A new dynasty, native or foreign, in Egypt, a revolution or a conquest in China, a new Germanic people in the Roman Empire, were elements in the history of the landscape like a change in the fauna or the migration of a flock of birds.

In the history, the genuine history, of higher men the stake fought for and the basis of the animal struggle to prevail is ever — even when driver and driven are completely unconscious of the symbolic force of their doings, purposes, and fortunes — the actualization of something that is essentially spiritual, the translation of an idea into a living historical form. This applies equally to the struggle of big style-tendencies in art (Gothic and Renaissance), of philosophy (Stoics and Epicureans), of political ideals (Oligarchy and Tyrannis), and of economic forms (Capitalism and Socialism). But the post-history is void of all this. All that remains is the struggle for mere power, for animal advantage *per se*. Whereas previously power, even when to all appearance destitute of any inspiration, was always serving the Idea somehow or other, in late Civilization even the most convincing illusion of an idea is only the mask for purely zoological strivings.

The distinction between Indian philosophy before and after Buddha is that the former is a grand movement towards attaining the aim of Indian thought by and in the Indian soul, and the latter the perpetual turning-up of new facets of a now crystallized and undevelopable thought-stock. The solutions are there, for good, though the fashions of expressing them change. The same is true of Chinese painting before and after the Han dynasties — whether we know it or not — and of Egyptian architecture before and after the beginning of the New Empire. So also with technics. The West's discoveries of the steam-engine and of electricity are accepted by the Chinese today in just the same way — and with just the same religious awe — as bronze and the plough were accepted four thousand years ago, and fire in a still remoter age. Both, spiritually, differ *in toto* from the discoveries which the Chinese made for themselves in the Chou period and which in each instance signified an epoch in their inner history. Before and after that time, centuries play a vastly less important rôle than decades and even years within the Culture, *for the spans of time are gradually returning to the biological order.* This it is that confers upon these very Late conditions — which to the people living in them seem almost self-evident — that character of changeless pageantry which the genuine Culture-man — e.g., Herodotus in Egypt and the Western successors of Marco Polo in China — has found so astonishing in comparison with his own vigorous pulse of development. It is the changelessness of non-history.

Challenge, Response, and Breakdown in China

ARNOLD J. TOYNBEE

Arnold J. Toynbee (b. 1889) was Professor of Greek language and history in the University of London from 1919 to 1955 and Director of Studies
in the Royal Institute of International Affairs from 1925 to 1955. In his study
of world history, China provides evidence in support of most of his famous
categories of historical growth and decay, which can only be listed here. China,
first, is the central site of two affiliated civilizations, the Sinic and the Far
Eastern. The Sinic progresses from genesis in a challenging environment through
growth, a universal state, and breakdown to disintegration. Barbarian invasions
and a universal church mark a transition to the affiliated civilization, the Far
Eastern, which follows a similar course to the point of disintegration, where,
however, it passes into a petrified existence.

Because Professor Toynbee's references to China are dispersed and often
brief, we reproduce only a few of the lengthier paragraphs, rearranged from
the original to follow each other chronologically, and to indicate his view of
China.

SINIC CIVILIZATION: GENESIS

If we consider . . . the genesis of the
Sinic Civilization in the lower valley of the
Yellow River we shall find a human response to a challenge from physical nature
which was perhaps even more severe than
the challenge of the Two Rivers and of
the Nile. In the wilderness which man
once transformed into the cradle of the
Sinic Civilization, the ordeal of marsh and
bush and flood was capped by the ordeal of
a temperature which varied seasonally between extremes of summer heat and winter cold. The fathers of the Sinic Civilization do not seem to have differed in race
from the peoples occupying the vast region
to the south and south-west which extends
from the Yellow River to the Brahmaputra
and from the Tibetan Plateau to the China
Sea. If certain members of that wide-spread
race created a civilization while the rest remained culturally sterile, the explanation
may be that a creative faculty, latent in all
alike, was evoked in those particular members, and in those only, by the presentation

of a challenge to which the rest did not
happen to be exposed. The precise nature
of that challenge is impossible to determine
in the present state of our knowledge.
What we can say with certainty is that the
fathers of the Sinic Civilization in their
home by the Yellow River did not enjoy
the fancied but delusive advantage of an
easier environment than their neighbours.
Indeed, none of the related peoples farther
south, in the valley of the Yangtse, for example, where this civilization did *not* origi-
nate, can have had so hard a fight for
life. . . .

Let us . . . consider the different degrees of difficulty presented by the lower
valleys of the two great rivers of China.
It seems that when man first took in hand
the watery chaos of the lower valley of the
Yellow River (Hwang Ho), the river was
not navigable at any season; in the winter
it was either frozen or choked with floating
ice, and the melting of this ice every spring
produced devastating floods which repeatedly changed the river's course by carving

From Arnold Toynbee, *A Study of History. Abridgement of Volumes I–VI* by D. C. Somervell,
pp. 74–505, selections. Copyright by the Oxford University Press, 1947. Reprinted by permission.

out new channels, while the old channels turned into jungle-covered swamps. Even to-day, when some three or four thousand years of human effort have drained the swamps and confined the river within embankments, the devastating action of the floods has not been eliminated. As recently as 1852 the channel of the Lower Hwang Ho was entirely changed and its outflow into the sea shifted from the southern to the northern side of the Shantung Peninsula, a distance of over a hundred miles. The Yangtse, on the other hand, must always have been navigable, and its floods, though they occasionally assume devastating proportions, are less frequent than those of the Yellow River. In the Yangtse Valley, moreover, the winters are less severe. Nevertheless, it was on the Yellow River and not on the Yangtse that the Sinic Civilization came to birth.

SINIC CIVILIZATION: BREAKDOWN AND UNIVERSAL STATE

If we turn . . . to the disintegration of the Sinic Society we shall identify the moment of breakdown with the disastrous collision between the two Powers Tsin and Ch'u in 634 B.C., and the moment of the establishment of the Sinic *Pax Oecumenica* with the overthrow, in 221 B.C., of Ts'i by Ts'in. If these are the two terminal dates of the Sinic time of troubles, are there any traces of a movement of rally-and-relapse in the intervening period? The answer is in the affirmative, for there is a perceptible rally in the Sinic time of troubles round about the generation of Confucius (*circa* 551–479 B.C.), inaugurated by the ultimately abortive disarmament conference of 546 B.C. Further, if we look at the history of the Sinic universal state, we find a notorious relapse and recovery in the interregnum, during the early years of the first century of the Christian Era, between the dynasties of the Prior and the Posterior Han. Again we find our three-and-a-half beats, the Sinic dates regularly occurring about two hundred years earlier than their Hellenic equivalents.

SINIC CIVILIZATION: VÖLKERWANDORUNG AND UNIVERSAL CHURCH

In the decline and fall of the Sinic Society "the triumph of Barbarism and Religion" is represented by the foundation of Eurasian Nomad successor-states of the Sinic universal state in the basin of the Yellow River round about A.D. 300, and by the simultaneous invasion of the Sinic World by the Mahayanian form of Buddhism, which was one of the religions of the Sinic internal proletariat in the northwestern provinces. But these triumphs, like those of "Barbarism and Religion" in the Roman Empire, were only victories of a moribund society's external and internal proletariats, and they constitute no more than the last chapter of the whole story. The Sinic universal state itself represented a social rally after a time of troubles in which the Sinic body social had been torn in pieces by fratricidal warfare between a number of parochial states into which the Sinic Society had previously articulated itself. The fatal date that, in the Sinic tradition, corresponds to the Hellenic 431 B.C. is 479 B.C., which is the conventional starting-point of what the tradition called "the Period of Contending States." Probably, however, this conventional date is some two hundred and fifty years later than the actual event, and has been taken as the beginning of the Sinic time of troubles simply because it is also the traditional date of the death of Confucius. . . .

The history of the Mahāyāna corresponds, so far as we have at present taken it, with that of Catholic Christianity in that both found their field of action in the Hellenic World instead of converting the non-Hellenic society from which each had sprung. But there is a further chapter in the history of the Mahāyāna to which the history of the Christian Church offers no parallel. For Christianity, having taken up its abode in the domain of the moribund Hellenic Society, remained there and ultimately survived to provide churches for the two new civilizations, our own and that of Orthodox Christendom, which have been affiliated to the Hellenic. The Mahāyāna, on the other hand, passed out through the ephemeral Hellenic Bactrian kingdom across the highlands of Central Asia into the moribund Sinic World, and, at a double remove from the land of its birth, became the universal church of the Sinic internal proletariat. . . .

FAR EASTERN CIVILIZATION:
STIMULUS OF NEW GROUND

. . . The Far Eastern Society . . . is affiliated to the Sinic Society. At what points in its domain has this Far Eastern Society shown the greatest vigour? The Japanese and the Cantonese stand out unmistakably as its most vigorous representatives to-day, and both these peoples have sprung from soil which is new ground from the standpoint of Far Eastern history. The southeastern seaboard of China was not incorporated into the domain of the "apparented" Sinic Society until a late phase of Sinic history, and even then only on the superficial plane of politics as a frontier province of the Han Empire. Its inhabitants remained barbarians. As for the Japanese Archipelago, the offshoot of the Far Eastern Civilization which was transplanted thither by way of Korea in the sixth and seventh centuries of the Christian Era was propagated there on ground that showed no trace of any previous culture. The strong growth of this offshoot of the Far Eastern Civilization on the virgin soil of Japan is comparable to the growth of the offshoot of the Orthodox Christian Civilization which was transplanted from the Anatolian Plateau to the virgin soil of Russia.

FAR EASTERN CIVILIZATION:
BREAKDOWN TO PETRIFICATION

. . . If we turn to the history of the main body of the Far Eastern Society in China, in which the moment of breakdown may be equated with the break-up of the T'ang Empire in the last quarter of the ninth century of the Christian Era, we can trace the subsequent process of disintegration following its normal course through a "time of troubles" into a universal state, only to be pulled up in the course of this stage by a reaction of the same abrupt and passionate kind as the Egyptiac reaction to the Hyksos invaders. The Southern Chinese revolt, under the leadership of the founder of the Ming dynasty, Hung Wu, against a Far Eastern universal state which had been established by the barbarian Mongols, is strongly reminiscent of the Theban revolt, under the leadership of the founder of the Eighteenth Dynasty, Amosis, against the "successor-state" which had been erected on part of the derelict domain of the defunct Egyptiac universal state (the so-called "Middle Empire") by the barbarian Hyksos. And there has been a corresponding similarity in the sequel. For the Far Eastern Society has prolonged its existence in a petrified form instead of passing expeditiously through disintegration into dissolution by way of a universal state running out into an interregnum.

III. MODERN CYCLICAL INTERPRETATIONS

The Periodic Recurrence of Internecine Wars in China

J. S. LEE

Modern attempts at periodization concentrating on Chinese history itself, often reflect both new and old influences. In the following selection, Professor J. S. Lee (Li Ssu-kuang, b. 1887) plots two great periods between the third century B.C. and the fifteenth of the Christian era, each with similar patterns of warfare. A third period, not yet completed, seems to follow the same development. The representation of the familiar Chinese theme of order and disorder in the shape of statistical measurements and curves suggests old wine in new bottles. Another hint of the old spirit seems to appear at the end of the essay, where Professor Lee, without attempting to explain the causes of the curves he has found, observes that the power of nature should be recognized.

Professor Lee has held many academic positions, including that of Director of the Institute of Geology, Academia Sinica. In the 1950's he was active in both academic and political organizations in the People's Republic and in 1958 joined the Chinese Communist Party.

THE notion of the periodic recurrence of certain major events in Chinese history, for instance, the rise and fall of dynasties, or the alternation of the periods of peace and war, is probably entertained by most Chinese who profess to know anything of their past. Such a notion, however vague in its nature, must have been wrought out by sheer experience from time immemorial. It may be a mere illusion, an illusion based on the pseudo-analogy of events and an inadequate conception of time, but, on the other hand, it may contain some truth, for experience often teaches man more effectively than anything else.

With a view to giving this idea a fair test the writer has recently made an attempt to extract certain predominant facts from the long record of a multitude of events in Chinese history, and to arrange them in a suitable time scale. It is obvious that the facts selected for our proposed treatment must be (1) well-defined in their nature, (2) capable of being readily rendered into a statistical series, and (3) indicative of the general state of national existence during the time covered. To comply with these requirements nothing would seem more suitable than the internecine wars that have occurred throughout China's history.

In times when the country is united or nominally united under the imperial system of government, a war waged within, no matter what be its magnitude, would involve the uprising of some determined force or forces that dare to defy the ruling authority. Again, when the imperial system disintegrates, there will be brought into play coexisting hostile forces that are liable to fling themselves against one another. In either case, the country and the people must be driven to such a state as to permit

From *The China Journal*, Vol. XIV, No. 3, 4 (March, April 1931), pp. 111–115, 159–163.

or favour the existence and activity of such force. We may, therefore, be able to gain some idea as to the condition of national life through the presence or absence of such hostile forces; and we can only know the existence of such forces through their action, the internecine war.

An internecine war on a large scale would undoubtedly produce greater material consequences than a minor one, but the state of disturbance staged thereby, or resulting therefrom, is not necessarily proportionally great. Often we read in Chinese history that great internecine wars are accompanied by local peace. In fact, without local peace, it would be impossible to organize a war on a large scale. The frequency of internecine war, irrespective of the magnitude, would thus seem to afford a measure of the state of peace or the degree of disturbance on the part of national life in general.

Inasmuch as we have a clear record of armed engagements in the past there is not much difficulty in counting the number of such open conflicts, but difficulty arises when we come to distinguish a true internal war from a war against alien peoples, for the issue hinges upon our interpretation of what is China and who are the Chinese people. We know, for instance, that China has grown from the Huang Ho Valley to the plain of Manchuria in the north and beyond the southern limit of the Si Kiang Valley in the south. As to the people a great confusion in our knowledge still prevails. From the point of view of those who assume themselves to be specimens of true Chinese the Miaos, Yaos, Lolos, Jews, Mohammedans, Mongols, Manchus and the like, that still maintain a community of their own within China, are undoubtedly foreigners, but, viewed from without, or from the national point of view, they are none the less Chinese, at least, for all practical purposes. Still more puzzling is the question of their diffused blood. The point cannot bear anthropological analysis. Fortunately anthropological analysis is not necessary for our present purpose. All that

which we need to define here is an expanse of land which constitutes China during historic times. China, as we generally understand it, is that geographical unit which embraces the drainage areas of the Huang Ho, the Yang-tze Kiang, the Si Kiang, the Liao Ho, one maritime province in the north, the Shantung Peninsula, and one in the south, comprising Southern Chekiang, Fukien and Eastern Kwantung. To these there are to be added the hilly region of Yunnan and a part of the semi-desert region in the north-west. The outline of this geographical unit was essentially laid down when the country was brought under the rule of the First Emperor of the Ch'in Dynasty over two thousand years ago. Peoples inhabiting these and adjacent areas were gradually forged into one mass by force of a distinctive culture, the Chinese culture, and adaptation to that culture means sinolization.

The process of adaptation has been a tedious and painful one. It meant wars, conquests, revolts and fresh wars until all the outstanding differences were worn out. We have to touch upon this point because, theoretically, it must affect our statistics regarding internal wars. Those wars which were fought between the generals of the Han Dynasty and the Hsiungnu, Hsienpei, Kiang and so on were obviously wars against alien peoples, for the northern tribes of those days were regarded by the then Chinese as barbarians, and they were no doubt culturally inferior. Moreover, the battles were largely staged on or far beyond the outskirts of China. Such wars cannot, therefore, be placed in the category of internal wars. Speaking in modern terms, they were wars waged either for imperialistic aggression or for national defense on the part of the Chinese. The same argument applies to the wars of the Han Dynasty against the south-western tribes . . . These peoples were presumably already under the strong influence of Chinese culture early in the Han Dynasty, but they resisted subjugation until they were repeatedly defeated by force of arms.

For these reasons the wars against the northern and south-western tribes during the Han Dynasty ought to be discarded from the list of internecine wars for that period. Even if we do take them into account they do not materially alter our statistics; for they were intermittent, sporadic and spread over a long period of time.

Coming down to the period of the Eastern Ch'in and the Six Dynasties there was a great influx of the northern peoples into North China. Some of them, notably the [Northern Wei], brought with them their own type of culture. On the whole, however, they did not come as complete strangers. Among them were numerous true Chinese, as genuine as any of the Chinese who then played a dominant rôle in the south. The wars waged among themselves or against the south cannot, therefore, be treated on the same basis as those fought between the Han Dynasty and the northern tribes. In other words, they were internecine wars. The same status must be assigned to the wars between the Southern Sung Dynasty and those peoples who occupied North China under the names of Liao and Kin. It would take too long to go through the historical evidence. Those who are familiar with the general history of the Southern Sung Dynasty would be compelled to admit that both the Liao and the Kin were highly sinolized peoples. There were probably as many Chinese elements in them as there were in the contemporary Southern Sung regime.

The Mongolian invasion was, however, a different thing. The Mongols were essentially barbarians from the north. They came to China as conquerors. They learnt very little from China before they decayed and were exhausted. The Manchus started as a small barbarian northern tribe; but they were sagacious enough to absorb Chinese culture even in the early stage of their adventure. They came to China more or less as foreigners, but they ruled China essentially as Chinese.

These considerations provide us with a guiding principle in determining the number of internecine wars within China for a particular period. Our criterion of prime importance is, of course, a geographical one. Racial and cultural complications are taken into account only in such times as when the geographical boundary becomes less obvious through foreign invasion on a large scale. Historical record, however, shows that the wars on the borderland, either in the actual or the virtual sense, were comparatively limited in frequency. That is, in times of profound internal peace, there might have been wars waged for national defense or expansion. We find typical cases of such wars in the Han, T'ang and other flourishing dynasties. Wars of that nature are not of frequent occurrence in comparison with those occurring in periods of internal upheaval. Again, in times of internal chaos, the number of unmistakable internecine wars for a given period generally rises to such a figure that an addition or deduction of a few battles of ambiguous nature would not materially affect the order of the statistical record. We have already laid some stress on this point in dealing with the wars of the Han Dynasty. The same argument, in fact, applies to all dynasties up to the present day.

Thus, guarding ourselves against any possible error in selecting the data, we may now proceed to deal with the various internecine wars recorded in Chinese history with a view to finding out whether they display any periodicity when arranged on a uniform time-scale. First of all we must fix, though necessarily arbitrarily, a definite time interval in which the number of internecine wars is to be counted. A period of five years is here chosen as the time-unit. The number of wars that occurred during this interval is then the frequency of internecine wars per five-year period. Any other interval would answer our purpose as well, but probably none could be more convenient.

Our statistical record starts with 221 B.C., namely, the year when the First Emperor of the Ch'in Dynasty unified the whole country. From this year on Chinese history presents a very clear record of wars of varying size. And this was the very year when the outline of China as a geographical unit was essentially established. Our record runs down to 1929 A.D., the eighteenth year of the Republic. Throughout this long span of time the number of internecine wars for every five years has been counted in succession, and the successive numbers plotted vertically on a uniform scale against a horizontal uniform scale of time. This results in the accompanying Internecine War Frequency Curve. . . .

* * *

Figures plotted on the diagram may not be absolutely accurate for any interval during those long years. That they are essentially correct cannot, however, be disputed. A more accurate survey would probably result in the accentuation of the disquieting parts of the curve, but there is no reason to expect any material alteration of its general form and successive order. It is the general form and successive order of the curve that is required to yield evidence of periodicity, if such does exist.

The lower curve is a mere diagrammatic representation of facts. It will be seen in this diagram that the peaks of the curve occur in groups of close connection. In order to simplify the matter, each group of peaks is lumped into one so as to render the salient features of the curve more easily legible and visualizable as indicated on the upper diagram. The latter is developed more or less as an "envelope" of the lower curve. It signifies the distribution of the periods of disturbances and their relative intensity, and thereby retains the essential features of the lower curve, but in a much more simplified form.

When we come to examine these curves, it will be seen at once that prolonged periods of peace do alternate with prolonged periods of disturbance. In so far as our diagrams go, the former periods are covered by the West and East Han, the Earlier and Later T'ang (probably including a part of the Northern Sung) and the Ming and

Ch'ing Dynasties. These periods are each followed by a period of successive disturbances with the exception, of course, of the Ming and Ch'ing, the following period of which is yet to be unfolded.

Each alternation of these long periods of peace and disturbance constitutes a cycle of the first order. Curiously enough, each of these cycles covers an approximately equal length of time. Thus the Ch'in-Sui Cycle (from A to B) stretches over some 820 years, and the Sui-Ming Cycle (from B to C) about 780 years. The Chou Cycle which precedes the Ch'in-Sui Cycle also covers a period of time not incomparable with the later cycles, being 874 years in length. The march of events during the Chou Dynasty, though not indicated in the diagram, is roughly of the same order. It witnessed a period of peace in its first part for some three to four hundred years; then followed a period of disturbance with increasing intensity, the Chunchiu and Chankuo Periods.

Such a broad comparison seems to be rather hazardous; for the parallelism may be coincidental. Further analysis of the curves, however, shows that coincidence far exceeds the limit of probability in this case. We need not go through the mathematical argument. A careful comparison of the different phases of the curve displayed by two complete cycles will render the parallelism indisputable and exact, perhaps too exact to be expected from the proceedings of human affairs.

It will be observed in the simplified diagram that there are altogether seven waves of disturbance in each cycle, namely from A to B and from B to C. The first wave (a or a') occurred soon after the commencement[1] of the cycle. It came in with some violence, but rapidly subsided. This was followed by a long period of quiescence. Then came the second concussion (b or b') again with considerable violence. A second long period of peace again ensued. As this

[1] The starting point of a cycle is, of course, conveniently chosen.

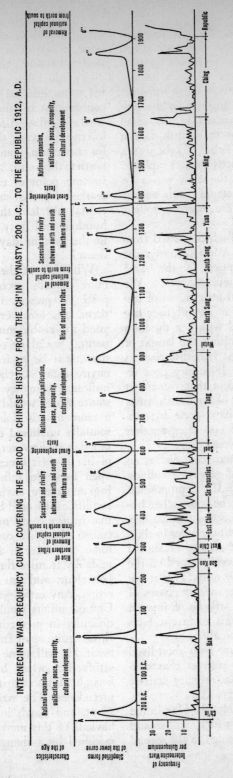

INTERNECINE WAR FREQUENCY CURVE COVERING THE PERIOD OF CHINESE HISTORY FROM THE CH'IN DYNASTY, 200 B.C., TO THE REPUBLIC 1912, A.D.

29

peaceful period drew towards its end, waves of disturbance appeared more or less in continual succession. The third wave (c or c') was a little more advanced in the Sui-Ming Cycle, but it is of much the same form as the corresponding one in the preceding cycle, and occurred in the same relative position. From the fourth to the seventh (d, e, f, g or d', e', f', g') the waves advanced with a distinctly greater rapidity. It is remarkable that the fifth waves (e and e') are, in both cases, of much smaller amplitude, and therefore afford a salient feature for correlation.

In the present cycle which started from the beginning of the Ming Dynasty, the curve behaves still much in the same manner as in the previous cycles. We have so far experienced four waves of disturbance (a'', b'', c'', d''), and they are significantly distributed within a duration which almost exactly equals the length of time covered by the first four disturbances in the previous cycles. If history does repeat itself, it would seem that we are at present just on the crest of the fourth wave. Peace and prosperity have gone by; disturbances will succeed one after another between intervals of ephemeral rest.

We have selected internecine war as an indicative factor of the general condition of national life in China. If this proposition be valid, there ought to be some other historical phenomena of some importance, which also display a rhythmic order in their manifestation, and which, moreover, should more or less follow the cycles based on the frequency of internecine wars. This is not the place to discuss the various phases of Chinese history; but it will be of interest to note certain important recurrent facts that may serve as corroboration.

The Ch'in and Sui are both short-lived régimes. They are both régimes characterized by iron rule, intense military activity and great engineering feats. . . .

The next period, namely, the Han in the first cycle, T'ang (to which we should perhaps add Northern Sung) in the second cycle, and Ming and Ch'ing in the present cycle, is one of peace, prosperity, national unification and cultural development. . . .

A gradual decay of these flourishing ages led to an internal disintegration with the concomitant and increasing activities of the northern tribes. After a period of chaos and internecine wars, the national capital was for one reason or another removed from the north to the south. . . . Measuring from the starting point of each cycle to the point marked by the shifting of the national capital, we find that there are some five hundred and forty years. This is true up to the present day. Is it a mere coincidence? . . .

What factors, then, contributed to determine China's peculiar behaviour in the past? At present we fail to understand them. It is, however, certain that forces beyond the visible must be at work, be they natural, social or economic. In any case, they must be profoundly connected with environment. Cyclic repetition generally indicates stagnancy of progress, a circumstance which would necessarily result from a more or less isolated existence and essentially unaltered environment. China of our day is, however, no longer the China of her historic times. By throwing herself open to world influences she is brought into a strange environment. Under such conditions it would be too much to suppose that history could not be made to alter its course through a conscious effort. But the force of nature is innate, grim and formidable. It rules the possibilities of man's behaviour, and sets limitations to his exertion. Any intelligent observer of modern Chinese affairs would probably have little difficulty in predicting China's immediate future quite apart from our historical argument. He will, none the less, find a quaint satisfaction when his own prediction is brought into comparison with historical precedence. The writer prefers to remain silent, and watch how far the innate behaviour of this marvellous people may be modified by a changed environment. . . .

The Dynastic Cycle

EDWIN O. REISCHAUER

Edwin O. Reischauer (b. 1910) was Professor of Far Eastern Languages at Harvard University and Director of the Harvard-Yenching Institute before he became Ambassador of the United States to Japan in 1961.

The book from which the following selection comes was written in collaboration with John K. Fairbank, Francis Lee Higginson Professor of History at Harvard and Director of the East Asian Research Center. Professor Reischauer presents a remodelled one-dynasty cycle, granting the traditional view centering around the emperor some validity as a "superficial political pattern," but seeing a more fundamental cycle in economic-administrative events.

THE DYNASTY CYCLE:
PERSONAL FACTORS

The Chinese practice of compiling the records of the past in dynastic chunks is partially responsible for the traditional interpretation of Chinese history as a series of repetitive dynastic cycles. The lack of a belief in progress and the idea that there was a golden age in antiquity have strengthened this tendency, for the most that could be expected of history as it unfolded was the repetition of past glories. As a result, the fascinating story of the growth of Chinese civilization has been made to seem like one vast human treadmill. After reading the story of one dynasty, the student may feel that the next is just more of the same.

The Han historians, with their assumption that ancient China had enjoyed the same imperial unity they knew, managed to hide many of the fundamental changes between Shang times and the early Han under a surface pattern of repetitive motifs. Later historians made the succeeding 2000 years seem an even more monotonous series of more or less successful attempts to repeat the story of the Earlier Han dynasty. The concept of the dynastic cycle, in other words, has been a major block to the understanding of the fundamental dynamics of Chinese history. Even today historians are only beginning to grope their way toward the establishment of such useful generalizations as are afforded in Western history by its division into ancient, medieval, and modern periods.

It must be admitted, on the other hand, that there is considerable validity to the Chinese concept of the dynastic cycle, if one interprets it as a somewhat superficial political pattern that overlay the more fundamental technological, economic, social, and cultural developments. The two Han dynasties each lasted about two centuries; the great dynasties of later times, existing under somewhat different sociological and technological conditions, each tended to last about three centuries. And within each dynasty such matters as fiscal conditions, administrative efficiency, and power relations with the "barbarians" followed remarkably similar patterns. In fact, the Chinese concept of the dynastic cycle, if applied to the more stable periods of history in other parts of the world, might be found to have a greater degree of general validity than the more sweeping theories of cultural cycles put forth by such Western historians as Spengler and Toynbee.

From Edwin O. Reischauer and John K. Fairbank. *East Asia: The Great Tradition.* (Boston, 1960), pp. 114–118. Reprinted by permission of Houghton Mifflin Company.

Chinese historians, influenced by the Confucian insistence on the ethical basis of government, have always emphasized personal factors in explaining the dynastic cycle. Founders of dynasties, who, like Kao Tsu, successfully claimed the Mandate of Heaven, were not portrayed just as strong men but as veritable supermen, if not demigods. The last rulers, who lost the Mandate, were not considered just unfortunate or weak but were often described as evil and debauched, like the last kings of the Hsia and Shang.

Actually, the imperial lines invariably degenerated. The dynastic founder naturally had to be a man of great ability and force, and his original drive was likely to carry on for a few generations. Later rulers, raised in a luxurious and intrigue-ridden court, were more likely to be weaklings. Usually the dynasty produced at least one later strong man who either brought the regime to new power, as did Wu Ti, or gave it a sort of second start; but in general all the imperial lines showed a downward trend in ability, particularly in their last century of rule.

The quality of the men around the throne was on the whole more important than that of the emperors themselves. Here the picture is less clear. Struggles over the succession and court intrigues between rival factions characterized the history of all the dynasties almost from beginning to end. In the latter years of a dynasty, when the central government was weakening for other reasons, such factional quarrels, coups d'état, and palace revolutions, however, were naturally more deleterious than in the dynasty's heyday.

Factional quarrels in Han times were for the most part simply struggles over power and rewards. A typical example is afforded by Ho Kuang, a half brother of the general Ho Ch'ü-ping. A faithful administrator, Ho Kuang dominated the court during the reign of Wu Ti's successor, but his power began to fade with the accession of Hsüan Ti (the "Comprehensive Emperor") in 74 B.C., and, shortly after Kuang's death

six years later, the whole Ho family was destroyed by its rivals.

In later dynasties . . . factional quarrels occasionally became more clearly ideological. Large factions, splitting the whole upper bureaucracy, sometimes feuded for generations over basic policy matters, thus impairing the efficiency of the central government far more than the briefer and more limited power struggles of earlier times.

One type of factional struggle that was endemic in all the dynasties was that between civil bureaucrats and eunuchs. The eunuchs naturally were at court to guard and administer the imperial harem, but their functions spread to other fields. As men of low social origin without descendants who could rival the imperial line, they were the natural allies of those emperors who sought to curb their more ambitious or greedy officials. The empresses, in particular, tended to rely on eunuchs, for these were the only men with whom they came in close contact in the harem. As a result eunuchs commonly came to hold high posts in the imperial household, and frequently they were made the commandants of the palace guards and in later dynasties even supervisors of the frontier armies.

The bureaucrats naturally looked with keen disfavor on these influential eunuchs, who lacked their own education, came from a different social background, and were their rivals for power and rewards at court. Since the writing of history was the prerogative of the more scholarly bureaucrats, we find the eunuchs uniformly condemned in the Chinese histories for their misrule. Whatever the truth of the matter, there can be no doubt about the bitter rivalry between eunuchs and bureaucrats. . . . Under the Ch'in . . . the eunuch Chao Kao did away with Li Ssu. In 47 B.C. we find another great eunuch getting rid of his rivals at court. The high point of eunuch power came in the second half of the Later Han dynasty, when they often completely dominated the court.

The most persistent factional problem

was that posed by the families of the empresses. . . . Kao Tsu's empress almost took the throne for the Lü family. Wu Ti had a characteristically drastic solution for the problem: he destroyed the relatives of the woman whose son he named as heir apparent. His successors were less ruthless, and within a century Wang Mang, the nephew of an empress, was able to take the throne for himself. The son of an empress of the Wang family ascended the throne in 33 B.C., and soon her relatives came to dominate the court. By 8 B.C. Wang Mang, who was already a marquis, had intrigued his way to the highest position in the bureaucracy. After a temporary eclipse during the reign of the next emperor, he emerged again as all-powerful in 1 B.C., dominated the government during the reigns of two children, and in 8 A.D. finally usurped the throne and established the Hsin (or New) dynasty.

THE DYNASTIC CYCLE: ECONOMIC AND ADMINISTRATIVE FACTORS

Despite the Chinese emphasis on the personal factor, it was by no means the chief element in the dynastic cycle. In fact, Wang Mang's usurpation is not the end of the first dynastic cycle, but rather the beginning of its last chapter — namely, the collapse of the Han central government that took place in his reign. A much more fundamental part of the story is the closely related rise and fall of the fiscal stability of the dynasty, its administrative efficiency, and its military power. The dynastic cycle, in other words, seems to be mainly an economic-administrative cycle, not a matter of personal character or genes.

All the great dynasties have an initial period of prosperity. The group that has seized the throne is relatively small and closely knit. The wars that have brought it to power have eliminated most of its rivals, and therefore the wealth of the nation pours largely into its coffers. The country prospers in its newly established peace, the population seems to increase rapidly, and the treasuries and granaries of the central government overflow.

But an excess of *yang* leads to the rise of *yin*. The affluent central government builds great palaces, roads, canals and walls. The imperial clan, the nobility, and the high bureaucracy grow in numbers and become accustomed to an ever more luxurious mode of life. The very military successes of the empire have established far-flung defense lines that are costly to maintain. More and more lands and their peasant-cultivators are used for the personal support of the ruling classes and fewer and fewer tax-paying contributors remain to the central administration. Because of constantly increasing expenditures and often a slight decline in income, each dynasty begins to experience serious financial difficulties within a century of its founding.

Economic and administrative reforms are then carried out and may halt the financial decline for a while. The downward trend, however, eventually reasserts itself. Economic and administrative difficulties accumulate. Official self-seeking and corruption become worse, leading to a decline in administrative efficiency and an intensification of factional quarrels at court. The potential rivals of the imperial family become politically and economically more independent of the central government and challenge it with greater impunity. To meet government deficits, the burden on the tax-paying peasant is increased to the breaking point. Because of the government's financial difficulties, canals and dikes are allowed to fall into disrepair, making floods and droughts more probable. Crop failures that once could have been offset by stores from the government granaries now result in famines, and these lead to banditry and eventually to peasant uprisings. Inadequately maintained frontier defenses begin to crumble. Provincial officials and their armies begin to defect, and the central government starts to go to pieces. Then follow the wars that liquidate the old regime and clear the slate for a new dynastic beginning.

Toward a Study of Dynastic Configurations in Chinese History

LIEN-SHENG YANG

Lien-sheng Yang is Professor of Chinese History at Harvard University. Assuming some validity in the idea of a pattern in the rise and fall of dynasties, he attempts in the following article to contribute toward more precise definitions of the repeated patterns, or "configurations," among dynasties. Though prepared to employ any modern concepts and superior viewpoints that would help to measure cultural achievement or quantify other components of a dynasty's life, he also commends use of the annals for a general picture of configuration and suggests that some traditional concepts, such as the division of forces in history between those of "Heaven" and of "Man," ought not to be rejected a priori. If the "multiple checking" he proposes showed a correlation among several aspects of the history of a dynasty, a one-dynasty period of rather precise character would appear. Even if marked configurations failed to emerge, he concludes, something useful would have been learned of the career of dynasties.

STUDENTS of Chinese history generally recognize in the rise and fall of dynasties a recurrent pattern which they call the dynastic cycle. Obviously a dynasty may experience a number of declines and revivals before the completion of its cycle. A detailed graph of a given cycle, taking account not only of the dynasty's general rise and fall but also of the minor ups and downs in between, may be termed a dynastic configuration. A study of such configurations, if they reflect fairly accurately what happened, will deepen our understanding of the dynastic cycle. The drawing of such a configuration, however, is no simple matter. I offer here some preliminary considerations of the major problems involved.

The first problem is: what are the dynasties to be included in our study? Chinese history is full of dynasties, long and short, Chinese and alien. The ruling houses which governed the whole or nearly the whole of China may be called major dynasties, and those which controlled only a portion of it, minor dynasties. When modern scholars speak of the dynastic cycle, they tend to refer to the cycles of major dynasties of considerable length; this may be justifiable, since obviously not all dynasties may be treated on the same basis. Nevertheless, it seems worthwhile to plot configurations for the minor dynasties in periods of disunity, including such independent states as the Seven Powers in the Period of Warring States and the Ten Kingdoms in south China during the Five Dynasties. It will be extremely interesting if one can correlate differences of configuration with differences in territory.

*   *   *

The second problem is: what are the beginning and end of a dynasty? Chinese tradition in general dates the beginning of a dynasty from the time when it declared a dynastic title, in most cases the declaration being in effect a claim to the mandate of Heaven. However, a dynasty may already have existed as a state before this official beginning. Such is the case of Ch'in, the first imperial dynasty, and on this score Ch'in differs widely from Sui, although the two dynasties are similar in several other ways. Early beginnings are also found in the alien dynasties and, as far as we can tell, the two very ancient dynasties, Shang and Chou. This similarity between alien and ancient Chinese dynasties is worthy of note. In our study it seems advisable to include the pre-"imperial" period of a dynasty, although one may wish to distinguish this part of the configuration from the rest somehow, e.g., by charting with different colors.

The end of a dynasty involves the interesting problem of *chung-hsing*, "revival or restoration." According to tradition, a revival may come after a complete break, such as the case of the Eastern Han, Eastern Chin, and Southern Sung. It may follow the pacification of a major rebellion. Thus after the rebellion of An Lu-shan, the T'ang dynasty was restored under Su-tsung (756–762), who was canonized as Hsüan Huang-ti, evidently to compare him with King Hsüan (827–782 B.C.) of the Chou dynasty who had achieved a revival. For the Ch'ing dynasty, people speak about the T'ung-chih restoration after the T'ai-p'ing rebellion. . . . Generally speaking, it is difficult to achieve a complete restoration and the revived phase tends to be less glorious than the earlier phase. The Eastern Han is probably the only exception.

Incidentally, the historical expression *chung-hsing* only means "revival" rather than "revival in the middle of a dynasty" as one might guess. . . .

In Chinese history there are cases when a dynasty is continued in a manner even short of a partial security, and for this precarious continuation its protagonists may still wish to claim a revival. A notable example is that of the Ming princes who established themselves in south China after the Manchu invasion, although what they actually accomplished was a brief survival rather than a revival. Revivals or survivals, it seems only fair for the historian to include them in the study of dynastic configurations, again bearing in mind the difference in territory. This applies to the alien dynasties as well as the Chinese. Thus the Khara-Khitai should be studied along with Liao, and the independent Mongolian princes in the Ming period may be considered survivals of Yüan.

The inclusion of both major and minor dynasties in our study, and also the pre-dynastic survivals, makes it necessary to consider configurations which overlap each other in time. The overlapping may be external or internal. Internal overlapping is typical in dynastic changes by way of abdication. First, the founder of the new dynasty, or his father, served as a powerful minister under the old dynasty. Finally, his influence became so overwhelming that the last ruler of the old dynasty was obliged to abdicate. This was the normal process of passing on the throne from the Han to the Sung dynasties inclusive. In such cases, we must be careful in our interpretation of the configuration of the old dynasty. For instance, toward the end of the two Han dynasties, there were signs that the central government had become strong, and these would be reflected in the configuration. But the strength was chiefly to the credit of Wang Mang and Ts'ao Ts'ao, who acted in the name of their masters. The upswing in the configurations indicates the rise of the Hsin dynasty and the Wei dynasty rather than a revival of Han.

External overlapping may exist between two dynasties, or among several dynasties or states, either Chinese or alien. In comparing their configurations, we may find factors which favored co-existence and factors which led to conquest. Obviously, one situation which has promoted co-existence is that in which two dynasties were both fairly strong and prosperous and had mutual respect for each other. The long peace between Northern Sung and Liao which lasted from 1004 to 1122 is an excellent illustration.

Old-fashioned Chinese scholars were inclined to study Chinese dynasties as isolated entities, and in their studies of relations with the non-Chinese states their views tended to be overly influenced by the key role played by China in East Asia. Fortunately, modern scholars have already been making attempts to correct this bias. In the West, works of Owen Lattimore and Karl A. Wittfogel are good examples. In China, Ch'en Yin-k'o in his brilliant volume on the political history of the T'ang dynasty has demonstrated the interlocking nature of the rise and fall of foreign races and the interaction between civil government and national defense. Students of Chinese history will do well in broadening their scope of study to include configurations of all non-Chinese states which had direct or even indirect contacts with China.

We come now to the third and perhaps the most important problem: what is the basis of grading or standard of measurements? Two obvious pairs of criteria are unity and expansion, and peace and prosperity, in other words, *wen-chih* and *wu-kung* or civil and military achievements. Of course, these two kinds of merit somehow contradict each other because unity and expansion often involves war, which is against peace. In general, Chinese tradition expects military merits from the founder of a dynasty, and civil achievements from his successors. . . . Expansionist emperors in the middle of a dynasty were often criticized for their ambition. For instance, after the death of Emperor Wu of Han, the court proposed to honor him with the temple name of *Shih-tsung* the "Epochal Exemplar." To this proposal, strong objection was raised by the classical scholar Hsia-hou Sheng who denounced the late emperor for the disasters which he had brought upon the people through his ambitious wars. Although this objection was not favorably received, it expressed the Confucianist view against expansion by force. An adequate national defense, however, was considered necessary. And when the character *wu* "martial" was used in an imperial designation, it was generally intended to be complimentary. For the purpose of showing the configuration, the modern student may draw two different curves based on the civil and military criteria, or one curve to indicate the average of the two. The use of two curves has its advantage. For instance, they may reveal a lag of the civil peak behind the military peak in the configuration, as suggested by the tradition which expects different kinds of achievements from dynasty-founders and from their successors.

Occasionally Chinese historians describe a glorious era in terms of cultural activities in such fields as philosophy, art and literature. Whether this is justifiable leads us to an interesting problem. Some years ago, the celebrated American anthropologist Alfred L. Kroeber made a study of configurations of culture growth and became rather disappointed at finding only a partial correlation between national solidarity and cultural achievement. On this highly complicated subject I wish to offer only a couple of general suggestions. First, there is the problem of defining the "culture" in culture growth. I believe, in making such a study, it may be useful to distinguish (1) a kind of cultural activity or a division of culture, such as poetry, (2) a particular form or genre in the division, such as *lü-shih* or regulated verse, and (3) cultural activities in general. The configurations of culture growth in these three senses need not coincide, as the causes of their rise and fall may vary.

Second, there is the problem of quantity and quality. Students in the history of art, literature, and philosophy chiefly concern themselves with quality rather than quantity. This approach may be adequate in their separate fields. For a full understanding of cultural history, however, we should like to learn not only about the best results achieved by the outstanding masters but also about the standard reached by the average work, and the total volume of achievements by all the participants in cultural activities. Generally speaking, although there are great masters who appear to have lived out of the period of their speciality (e.g., Bach and polyphony), the history of art, literature and philosophy reveals a rather close correlation between quality and quantity. For instance, in Chinese literature, tradition associates *fu* or rhymed prose with Han, *lü-shih* or regulated verse with T'ang, *tz'u* or song-words with Sung, and drama with Yüan. These are believed to be the periods that produced the most and the best. This correlation is understandable since the period that produced the most had a good chance to produce the best.

Whether a division of culture is especially favored or disfavored in a given society, and developed early or late in history, involves many factors — material as well as ideological — which can not be easily generalized. The rise and fall of a particular form in a cultural division can be interpreted to some degree by what I call a game theory. A particular form of art or literature is subject to a set of rules just like any competitive game which requires skill. Under the rules there are a limited number of possibilities to be realized by the player. Those who realize the best possibilities become the outstanding masters. Of course, those are also outstanding who invent a new game with many possibilities or modify an old game to make it more interesting. When people have exhausted the possibilities, or at least the good possibilities, the game (or the form of art or literature) will decline.

This point of exhaustion of possibilities has already been made by the seventeenth-century scholar Ku Yen-wu. His famous *Jih-chih lu* contains the following remarks on "Shih-t'i tai-chiang" ["Periodical Changes in the Style (or Form) of Poetry"]:

That the Three Hundred Poems (i.e., the *Shih ching*) had to be replaced by the *Ch'u*

tz'u, the *Ch'u tz'u* replaced by the poetry of Han and Wei, and in turn replaced by the poetry of the Six Dynasties and that of Sui and T'ang was natural. To follow the style (or form) of a period requires resemblance to the literature of that period — this is called conformation. That poetic and prosaic literature was different from period to period had a reason which made the change unavoidable. When the literary style of an era has been followed from a long time, it becomes intolerable for everybody to echo the same word. Now history has passed thousands of years; how can one imitate all the worn-out expressions of the past and still call the result poetry! Therefore, if one's work is [entirely] dissimilar to those of the ancients, it misses being poetry. On the other hand, if it is [entirely] similar to works of the ancients, it misses being one's own work. That the poetry of Li Po and Tu Fu was particularly outstanding among T'ang authors was because their poetry succeeded in being both similar and dissimilar [to traditional poetry]. He who understands this principle can be called a critic of poetry.

In Kroeber's *Configuration of Culture Growth* (p. 763) we also read, "The value culmination comes at the moment when the full range of possibilities within the pattern is sensed. . . . The pattern can be said to have fulfilled itself when its opportunities or possibilities have been exhausted." It may be observed that although this principle of exhaustion of possibilities can be applied to either a whole division of art or literature or to a particular form or style within the division, it is more effective when applied to the latter.

This is illustrated by Ku Yen-wu's discussion quoted above. The modern scholar Wang Kuo-wei made a similar observation and added, "Hence I dare not believe the remark that literature of later times is inferior to that of earlier times. But in speaking about one style (or form) of literature, this theory is irrefutable." In other words, the opportunities within a given poetic form or style are limited, whereas the possibilities of poetry as a whole appear to be too numerous to be exhausted.

Normally it takes a peaceful and prosperous era to permit many people to devote themselves to art and literature.[1] But whether they wish to play one game or another is a different proposition. Consequently, the correlation is likely to be only partial between the dynastic configuration and a culture configuration which represents a division of art or literature or a style or form within the division. As for cultural activities in general, in terms of quantity if not quality, at least in China there seems to be a considerable correlation between their high points and the peaks in the dynastic configuration. The period of Warring States is sometimes cited as a major exception to this thesis, because cultural activities were abundant in that period of disunion. But the correlation will immediately become clear if we ignore the royal house of Chou and turn our attention to the Seven Powers. When the terms of reference are clearly defined, it becomes possible to include in the civil criterion various cultural achievements. . . .

With our criteria defined, we may proceed to obtain a general picture of the configuration first by reading through the annals of the standard histories. The historian's comments at the end of an annal, known as *lun-tsan*, not infrequently discuss the emperor's position in the history of the dynasty. Such discussions are often stereotyped in form. Nevertheless, they are important because they represent a traditional evaluation. The following comments paraphrased from the *Hsin T'ang shu* may serve as examples:

On T'ai-tsung (627–649): Among the twenty rulers of the T'ang dynasty, three are remarkable. Of the three, Hsüan-tsung (713–755) and Hsien-tsung (806–820) both failed in the last part of their reigns. So outstanding was T'ai-tsung's greatness!

On Tai-tsung (763–779): In the reign of Tai-tsung, there were still remnant rebels. Able to complete the suppression and to maintain the accomplishment, he may be considered a ruler of medium caliber.

On Hsüan-tsung (847–859): Hsüan-tsung excelled in his judgment of affairs. But he relied too much on his fault-finding ability and completely lacked the spirit of benevolence. Alas! The T'ang dynasty began to decline from his time.

On Chao-tsung (889–903): In history the last ruler of a dynasty was not necessarily stupid or tyrannical. When the causes of disaster had accumulated for a long time and the time of collapse happened to occur in his days, even a wise and brave ruler could not save the situation. What a pity! Chao-tsung was such a case.

In apparent imitation of these passages, the *Ming shih* observes that among the sixteen Ming rulers, outside of T'ai-tsu (1368–1398) and Ch'eng-tsu (1408–1424), only Jen-tsung (1425), Hsüan-tsung (1426–1435) and Hsiao-tsung (1488–1505) are remarkable. In the annals, Ming Shih-tsung (1522–1566) is labeled a ruler of medium caliber and Emperor Chuang-lieh (1628–1644) is lamented exactly as was the last ruler of T'ang.

The traditional historian occasionally comments on the appropriateness of the posthumous imperial designation. For instance, the *Sung shih* remarks that in Jen-tsung's (1023–1063) benevolence and Hsiao-tsung's (1163–1189) filial attributes, they certainly lived up to their temple names. The *Sung shih* also approves the temple name Li-tsung (1225–1264) as suitable because the emperor made great efforts to promote the Neo-Confucianist thinking called *li-hsüeh*. Such remarks on appropriateness are relatively few, obviously because the eulogistic words used in the imperial designations were in most cases excessive and cannot be taken literally. To grasp the true meaning of a temple name, it is sometimes necessary to check the precedent usages in earlier dynasties. For

---

[1] This traditional view should not be considered one-sidedly materialistic, because the Chinese tradition also recognizes the principle of challenge and response, e.g., as expressed in the saying "Wen ch'iung erh hou kung" — "One's literary writings excel only after experience of poverty (or hardships)," or as expressed in more general terms in *The Works of Mencius* (Legge, *The Chinese Classics*, Vol. II), pp. 447–448.

instance, Sung Shen-tsung (1068–1085) and Ming Shen-tsung (1573–1619) are comparable because each of the two emperors trusted a minister who introduced reforms. Under the Ch'ing dynasty, had the Hundred-Day Reform in 1898 been more successful, the Kuang-hsü emperor might have received the temple name Sheng-tsung rather than that of Te-tsung.

Concerning the imperial career, tradition recognizes a close relationship between successful emperors and long-lived emperors. This tradition goes back to the chapter "Wu-i" "Against Luxurious Ease" in the *Book of Documents,* in which the Duke of Chou is reported to be addressing King Ch'eng. In the address, references are made to three Shang kings who restored the glory of the dynasty from a preceding low ebb, and who reigned for seventy-five, fifty-nine and thirty-three years respectively. The Sung scholar Su Che expressed doubts about such a correlation for later periods, pointing to such rulers as Liang Wu-ti (502–551) and T'ang Hsüan-tsung (712–756) as examples of long reigns which ended in disaster. However, another Sung scholar, Shao Yung, noted with pride and satisfaction that the first four Sung emperors together actually reigned as long as a century. On the whole, there seems to be a rather close correlation between a long reign and success, because in most cases at least a part of the long reign did constitute a peak in the configuration.

The importance of long reigns applies to alien dynasties as well. "Of the rulers of the Liao dynasty," says the *Liao shih,* "Sheng-tsung (983–1030) was about the only one who enjoyed a lengthy reign and lasting fame." For the Chin dynasty, the glorious reigns were those of Shih-tsung (1161–1189) and Chang-tsung (1190–1208). As described by the poet Yüan Hao-wen, "During the fifty years of Ta-ting (1161–1189) and Ming-ch'ang (1190–1195) [etc., the emperors'] godlike merits and sage virtues filled three (i.e., several) thousand documents." For the Ch'ing dynasty, students are familiar with the fact

that the three periods of K'ang-hsi, Yung-cheng, and Ch'ien-lung covered a record length of 134 years (1662–1795). Although it is normal for a dynasty to have an early peak in its configuration, this early plateau is extraordinary. This long period of consolidation and expansion undoubtedly helped to make the Ch'ing dynasty a stable and lasting dynasty of conquest.

Corresponding to the relationship between long reigns and success, traditional historians also associate short reigns with decline. The length of a reign and that of a dynasty is difficult to interpret, because the factors involved tend to be numerous and complicated. In traditional terms, the factors were often vaguely grouped into those belonging to *T'ien* "Heaven, or Nature" and those belonging to *Jen* "Man." The human factors cited in tradition are usually based on common sense and consequently are easy to understand. The *T'ien* factors, however, are rather slippery for comprehension, often in terms of such semi-mystical concepts as the Five Elements, *ch'i-yun* "vitality and fortune" or *ch'i-shu* "vitality and number."

Traditional interpretation of these concepts may be naturalistic or mechanical. The compounds *ch'i-yun* and *ch'i-shu* are often synonymous, but the character *shu* "number" in *ch'i-shu* in itself suggests a mechanical view expressed in figures. Perhaps the most famous example is the remark by Mencius, "It is a rule that a true royal sovereign should arise in the course of five hundred years, and during that time there should be men illustrious in their generation." But the most gigantic scheme is probably that of Shao Yung,[2] which covers not only cycles of mankind but also that of the universe, which was supposed to last 129,600 years. . . . A lesser known scheme of somewhat smaller scale is one invented by Wang Po in the seventh century. According to Wang, the dynasty

[2] For a description of Shao's scheme, cf. Fung Yu-lan, *A History of Chinese Philosophy,* trans. by Derk Bodde, Vol. 2 (1953), pp. 469–476.

that had the Earth Power (or Virtue) should last a thousand years, that which had the Metal Power should last nine hundred years, the Water Power six hundred years, the Wood Power eight hundred years, and the Fire Power seven hundred years. The Yellow Emperor had the Earth Power, and the cycle started by his reign was completed with Han, which had the Fire Power. The minor dynasties after Han should not count, and the T'ang dynasty should begin another cycle with its Earth Power and should last a thousand years. To a modern student, such mechanical schemes undoubtedly will sound ridiculous.

The following observation by the Ch'ing scholar Chao I seems to derive from the concept of ch'i-yün ("vitality and fortune"), in a rather eloquent application. How far his views can be endorsed is of course another matter. The topic of his discussion was: "Most Emperors of the Eastern Han Failed to Live Long."

When the "vitality and fortune" of a dynasty were excellent, the rulers in general lived long, had sons early, and had many of them. The case of the Eastern Han dynasty, however, was not so. Emperor Kuang-wu lived to the age of sixty-two, Emperor Ming forty-eight, Emperor Chang thirty-three, Emperor Ho twenty-seven, Emperor Shang two, Emperor An thirty-two, Emperor Shun thirty, Emperor Ch'ung three, Emperor Chih nine, Emperor Huan thirty-six, and Emperor Ling thirty-four. Prince Pien came to the throne at seventeen, and in the same year was murdered by Tung Cho. Only Emperor Hsien, after his abdication, survived until 234 when he died 'at the age of fifty-four. These were the ages of the emperors. Since the rulers did not live long, their successors certainly would be still young. When a young ruler died without heir, if there was already a dowager empress serving as his regent, she naturally would wish to put a small child on the throne in order to continue her control. . . .

In general, the peak of Han was in the period when its capital was in the west at Ch'ang-an. Coming down to the time of Emperors Yüan and Ch'eng, the "vitality and fortune" already began to decline. Therefore, when Emperor Ch'eng died without heir,

Emperor Ai was called in to succeed him. When Emperor Ai died without heir, Emperor P'ing was called in to succeed him. When Emperor P'ing died without heir, Wang Mang put the young prince Ying on the throne. This is what Pan Ku in his history referred to in saying that "three times the national lineage was broken." Emperor Kuang-wu was a descendant of Liu Fa, Prince Ting of Ch'ang-sha, and originally belonged to a collateral line. The case may be compared to that of a tree-trunk several hundred years old, which suddenly issued a new bough. Though the bough might appear extremely flourishing, its vitality was already limited. When branches grew from this bough, they would be still smaller, weaker, and more easily broken. After Chin moved south, most rulers came to the throne when young. After Sung moved south, also there were many cases when outside princes were called in to succeed to the throne. These were caused by a decline in "vitality and fortune" and could not be controlled by human efforts.

Chao's interpretation of vitality and fortune was naturalistic rather than mechanical, and while relying heavily on the T'ien factor he did not ignore the human side of the picture. For instance, his point on the selfishness of dowager empresses was based on human psychology.

In another passage where he discussed the many young rulers of Chin, he repeated the same thesis of vitality and fortune, but also added, "Nevertheless, the Eastern Chin dynasty lasted eighty to ninety years. That was through reliance on the assistance of the great ministers." This is a good point; in the above discussion we may have over-emphasized the role played by the emperor, but not by intention. We start with the imperial annals because they provide us with a short survey. The emperor serves as a focusing point but need not occupy our whole attention. Obviously there were emperors in history who were mere figureheads. And of course even the most energetic emperor could not govern a vast empire like China single-handed.

The general picture obtained from a

reading of the annals may or may not be accurate. To ensure some degree of reliability, the rough configuration should be subjected to what may be called multiple checking. As far as possible, information should be found concerning the territory, the number, intensity and results of foreign and civil wars, the population, the cultivated land, works for water conservancy, the currency, the price level, the number and intensity of natural calamities and the efforts made to meet such a challenge, the number of successful and unsuccessful candidates in the civil service examinations, the number of able ministers and benevolent administrators, etc.

A few studies along such lines have been made by modern scholars, for instance, in the study on internecine wars by Li Ssu-kuang, on water works by Chi Ch'ao-ting, on land tax by Wang Yü-ch'üan, on floods and droughts by Yao Shan-yu, on price levels in T'ang and Sung times by Ch'üan Han-sheng, and on portents during the Western Han period by Bielenstein and Eberhard. The works by Ch'üan, Bielenstein and Eberhard are especially interesting because they represent the first serious attempts to draw configurations under single dynasties based on one criterion. It is true that many figures in Chinese historical works cannot be accepted at their face value. For instance, population figures and land acreage tended to have fiscal significance rather than reflecting the real situation. Reports on portents and calamities may have been omitted or fabricated. But in many cases such figures can be made meaningful. Handled with care, they are by no means non-touchables.

In general, the above-mentioned and other modern studies have made contributions in advancing interpretations on the basis of geographical areas and social groups — in other words, on the stage and actors of history. These factors were not unknown in the Chinese tradition, but their effective use in historical interpretation is relatively new. Traditional scholars tended to identify a dynasty with the whole country and also with all classes. Nominally this may be true, but actually a dynasty was likely to have its basis in certain areas and certain groups of people. Further, these were the first things the dynasty would attend to, although it also had an interest in holding the empire. In this sense, a dynasty may be considered a composite entity of geographical and social forces. The interests in the capital and at court may be different from local interests. For instance, a decline of central control often means more freedom for the local rich and powerful. Also such matters as whether the political center and the economic center coincide have great influences over institutions of the dynasty. As for social groups, it is useful to keep in mind a distinction between the ruling classes and the ruled, the gentry and the peasantry, the civil and the military groups, etc. The presence of geographical and social differences, however, provides chances both for conflict and for cooperation. It is the duty of the historian to find out how the cooperative and conflicting forces worked under a dynasty. The study of dynastic configurations naturally leads one to the problem.

*   *   *

Only after making all the necessary checkings can we compare and interpret the different configurations intelligently. Only then can we tell in what sense Chinese history from dynasty to dynasty has been a repetition of the same cycle or different cycles. If we are contented with the thesis that the rise and fall of a dynasty involve both cyclical and non-cyclical factors (not necessarily those of *T'ien* and *Jen*), it is still desirable to find out the relative importance of the two types of factors for each dynasty. Otherwise, to speak about the dynastic cycle without going into the configurations would be too abstract to be useful. Dynasties rise and fall just as man is mortal. What is important is to learn something useful from the achievements and failures, in other words the careers, of mortal dynasties.

Periodization: Chinese History and World History

H. T. LEI

In the following selection, Professor H. T. Lei (Lei Hai-tsung, 1902–1962) proposes a periodization meant to be based independently on Chinese history, not on the model of European history. He finds two "cycles" in China, the first like that of other civilizations and the second unique. In achieving his distinctive periodization he has used some familiar European concepts. His periods, for example, are progressive, not "cycles," in that history never returns to the same phase; the characterization of any period seems to lie in the spirit of the "culture" of the time; and some of the phases occur similarly throughout the world. Politically and socially, he observes, Chinese civilization underwent no essential changes from Ch'in-Han times to the nineteenth century.

H. T. Lei was Professor of History in Tsing Hua University in the 1930s and '40s and was head of a world history teaching research group in Nankai University in 1957.

THE problem of periodization is one generally disposed of in quite a cavalier manner. Manuals of methodology or introductions to general history often contain some paragraph as follows:

Historical change is continuous; periodization is a matter of convenience, of relative, not absolute value. When we make a certain date the dividing line between two eras, it does not mean that the year before and that year after are absolutely different and distinct in character; in fact, even decades before and after the so-called line of demarcation, perhaps only very faint differences are perceptible. Keeping this in mind, we may without too much misgiving divide history into three ages: ancient, medieval, and modern.

All this is perhaps quite true, but it misses the mark entirely. History, if it is to mean anything, is change; the study of history is an attempt at an understanding of change and development. Without periodization, we can hardly expect to grasp the historical scene adequately. The universal neglect of this fact is largely responsible for the unsatisfactory ways of periodization prevalent in the field of history. Very few students in the Occident can escape from the spell of the threefold division of Western history or even universal history, and in this country we are only too apt to adopt Western fashions. Some of our countrymen, however, congratulate themselves for their discovery of five or six ages in Chinese history: most ancient, middle ancient, recent ancient, recent past, modern, and contemporary. The only thing we can say is that some people are ingenious in coining names.

Confucius once made the rectification of terms the pivot of his philosophy. The study of history, both in China and the West, certainly needs very badly a strict rectification of terms. The orthodox way of threefold periodization is a product of the Renaissance. The Humanists were becoming more and more antagonistic to the religious culture of the last millenium and beginning to feel themselves akin to the Greeks and Romans of old. They called the literary heritage of Greece and Rome Classics, and regarded their own age as

From *The Chinese Social and Political Science Review* XX (1935–1938), pp. 461–491.

one of the revival of these Classics, or Ren-aissance. The age between the Classics and the revival was a barbarous, especially Gothic era, sometimes contemptuously called in plural "the Dark Ages." It was a dark interlude between two ages of en-lightenment, a Medieval Age. The two ages of light they called Classical Antiquity and the Modern Age respectively. "Mod-ernity," however, hardly had the same con-notation as to-day; it meant a new age of Classicism, a revival of learning, a return to the good old days. . . .

*   *   *

This dubious procedure of the West has unwittingly been adopted in this country. Ever since the latter part of the nineteenth century we have been racking our brains to fit Chinese history into the Western scheme. Some divide Chinese history into three ages in the orthodox Western fashion, while others, perhaps sensing the unnatu-ralness of the scheme, try to overcome the awkwardness by a more minute division, believing themselves to have discovered five or six epochs in the history of our country. This can hardly be satisfactory.

*   *   *

. . . The various cultures being sepa-rate and independent, the object of perio-dization must be the individual civilizations, not Civilization, or Mankind, or the World. We must first make it clear in our mind the space-time limits of each individual culture before we can really proceed with the task of an intelligent understanding of history. The various cultures may be compared with one another, but funda-mentally they must be treated each by it-self. Let us take China as an example, di-vide its history into periods, and see if we can obtain some new light in comparing it with the other cultural areas of the world.

II

Chinese civilization may be said to have undergone two cycles. The first cycle, from the dim beginnings to 383 A.D., is that of Classical China, during which the race remained comparatively pure and its culture indigenous, with only slight and insignificant cultural infiltrations from without. The second cycle, from 383 A.D. to the present, is that of Tartar-Buddhist China (if we may coin a new term), char-acterized by repeated conquests of the coun-try by peoples from the north and by the gradual transformation of the classical civil-ization by Buddhism into a new synthesis, which, though still essentially Chinese, ex-hibits a rather thick veneer of the alien culture.

Let us take up the first cycle. The ori-gins of the ancient Chinese is still an in-soluble problem. All that we can say with certainty is that by 2000 B.C. the ancestors of the future Chinese were already inhabit-ing the Yellow River valley, and through-out the First Cycle this region was the center of Chinese history and civilization, with the Yangtze valley as a sort of politi-cal and cultural appendage, while the Pearl River valley came into the sphere of Chinese influence only at the end of the cycle. The first cycle, after the obscure ages of prehistory, may be divided into five periods:—

(1) The Feudal Age, 1300–771 B.C.;
(2) The Ch'un-ch'iu or Spring and Au-tumn Age, 770–473 B.C.;
(3) The Chan-kuo or the Age of the Contending States, 473–221 B.C.;
(4) The Empire, 221 B.C.–88 A.D.;
(5) The Fall of the Empire and the De-cay of Classical Civilization, 89–383 A.D.

*   *   *

[Around 771 B.C.] the royal domain of the west was completely overrun by the barbarians, and the new King, P'ing Wang (770–720 B.C.), was forced to abandon his ancestral patrimony and to go and stay at the eastern capital, Loyi (near the modern Loyang), for good. The feudal empire was shattered beyond recall; a new age, the

Ch'un-ch'iu, was ushered in, with the feudal states occupying the centre of the arena, while the King became a mere figurehead.

The religious beliefs of the feudal age were similar to those of all ancient peoples. Every important phenomenon of nature was personified into a god and devoutly worshipped. There were the rain god, the god of wind, the lord of thunder, the god or goddess of marriage, the spirit of the wayside, the divine husbandman, the god of the Kitchen, the divine archer, the powerful Count of the Yellow River, and a host of other divinities. Above all these was a supreme god, Shang Ti the lord on High, also known as Heaven or T'ien who was the lord of all gods and men. And symmetrical with this Lord on High was the Lord of the Earth.

The divine and the human were not very clearly differentiated. All the dead, at least the dead of the noble class, automatically became gods in heaven and were duly worshipped by their descendants, though, as a rule, only the recent dead were honoured with ceremonies, while the remote ancestors were allowed to pass into oblivion.

With the transfer of the capital to the east, the King no longer played the central role in history. An international system of states, with its corresponding world politics and struggle for hegemony, arose out of the last few centuries of feudal turmoil. All these states, big and small, still recognized the nominal overlordship of the King of Chou, whose only function, however, was to confer the Hegemonic title on whichever state that was able for a time to dominate the petty principalities of the centre. . . .

All these states had become more or less unified. The old feudal nobility was still in existence, but it had to play a subordinate part under the prince who was now supreme within the state. The common people still had nothing to do with politics; under the prince, the nobles retained their exclusive political control. But conditions varied in the various states. In Ch'in and Ch'u, for instance, feudalism had practically disappeared, while in Tsin the nobles were still so powerful as to make it a semi-feudal state.

*　　　*　　　*

Religion comprised the whole of the spiritual life of the feudal age, and seems to have continued to be the predominating influence through most of the Ch'un-ch'iu. But the closing decades of the age were a period of revolution and suffering and, as a result, saw the rise of the first glimmerings of rationalistic speculation. The philosophers, perhaps mostly sprung from the privileged class, diverged into three types. First, there were those who led in the overthrow of the old order, typified by Teng Hsi (d. 501 B.C.). Secondly, there were the pessimists who believed the situation hopeless and decided to save themselves by fleeing the world; of such recluses Confucius met quite a number during his wanderings. The third type was represented by the great Sage himself, who worshipped the age that had passed or was passing and devoted himself to preaching a return to the good old days.

The century after the fall of Wu in 473 B.C. was one of continuous political and social upheaval. . . . All became centralized states; the hereditary nobility and its prerogative of exclusive political control by the side of the prince were completely overthrown, and the prince from now on was to be an absolute despot. All political positions were at the disposal of the princely favour; no one was to hold any position by right. All were now, nominally at least, equal before the law. Whereas formerly the nobility had formed the major portion of the army, now, with the attainment of political and social equality, conscription came to be the recognized way of enlistment. Former wars had been comparatively harmless affairs, but now every state encouraged its citizen-soldiers to do their worst in the battlefield. In fact, a regular system was set up by which soldiers were rewarded according to the number of heads they could bring to their general.

The era of the Contending States, the most bloody in Chinese history, was also the golden age of philosophy. Though abstract thought was highly developed, yet the main theme of all schools may be said to be practical: one and all wanted to solve the pressing problem of political and social anarchy of this age of blood and to set forth a plan for the unification or, at least, pacification of the world. The solutions offered were of two categories: passive and active. Schools of the former type, the Taoists, the Dialecticians, and the school of Yang Chu perhaps more or less influenced by the pessimists of the end of the Ch'un-ch'iu, regarded the whole situation as irremediable and advocated only personal development and individual salvation. The latter type, the Confucians, the Micians, the Legists, and the Yin Yang school, imitated Confucius in ardently offering cures for all the ills of the world. All these schools, with the possible exception of the Legists, however, were rather doctrinaire, utterly ineffective against force and might, which ultimately pacified and unified the war-torn world in the person of Ch'in Shih Huang-ti 221 B.C.

For the first time in history China was organized into one state by Ch'in, and for the next two thousand years unity was to be the normal condition and disunity only temporary. Imperial unity was consolidated by the Ch'in and Han within the three centuries from 221 B.C. to 88 A.D. thus laying the institutional foundations of the next two millenniums. The proper territorial limits of China were also set up in this period.

Socially China was also given a permanent form by the Han dynasty. The clan system of society, all-important in feudal and Ch'un-ch'iu times, seems to have been considerably weakened, though not totally destroyed, by the Contending States, which had attempted to break up the clans in order to augment individual loyalty to the state. But now, with the passing of the age of incessant warfare, the temporarily overshadowed system of clans tended to reassert itself. At the same time, the emperor, looking around for a permanent support for the throne, set his eyes on the great landholders, among whom the clan system seems to have remained strongest. And with the establishment of Confucianism as the state religion, the fortune of the ancient social order may be said to have been assured, for that school was always harping back to the good old days of feudalism. And this resuscitated semi-feudal social system was also destined to last for two thousand years.

With the establishment of the universal empire, the conflicting schools of thought showed a steady decline in creativeness and influence. In fact, all schools tended to disappear except Confucianism, Taoism, and the Yin Yang, which one and all took on a more and more religious colour. Confucianism was recognized as the state cult, and Confucius, though never deified, was converted into a rather mystical personage. Taoism came to be a belief in the transmutation of metals and the elixir of life and all sorts of charms and other superstitions. As for the Yin Yang, it was more a pervasive influence than a sect. It never acquired a definite form or a concrete organization, but both Taoism and Confucianism were considerably influenced by it, and the whole atmosphere of belief and speculation during Han times was permeated by the ideas of Yin and Yang, the five elements, signs of fortune and misfortune, lucky and unlucky days, etc. And these beliefs, together with the two organized sects, were to form the basis of Chinese spiritual life down to the nineteenth century.

The reign of Ho-ti (89–105 A.D.) was an important period of transition. For fully three centuries before this, with one or two exceptions of very short duration, the empire had been consistently unified and strong, but with Ho-ti it began to decline, and permanently. The internal situation became increasingly untenable, while the barbarian pressure was more and more serious, till finally all the provinces along the northern frontier became practically barbarian territory. Meanwhile, the military spirit was also waning, and by the time of Ho-ti the Chinese army had become largely a barbarian force. Repeated internal insurrections and barbarian invasions shook the empire to its foundations, finally dissolving it into over half a dozen fragments. After the short period of the Three Kingdoms (208–263 A.D.), the Tsin dynasty again managed to unify the empire, but not for long.

Before describing the final catastrophe, however, let us review briefly the spiritual conditions of the age. Confucianism came to be an ossified system of pedantic erudition and dry ceremonial, with no inspiration for the people or even for the intellectuals. The independent spirits among the latter inclined toward a decadent sort of Taoism, known as Pure Discourse, which only served as an excuse for their nihilistic behaviour, denying all the ritual and moral code of Confucianism, drinking to excess, ridiculing and even insulting the people of the world in every possible manner, and in general doing anything and everything that their own sweet will might dictate. Such a philosophy of reckless decadence could neither be understood nor afforded by the common people, who found their comfort in a much baser brand of Taoism, which in the second century A.D. crystallized into a Taoist Church. It was in such an age of despair and unrest that Buddhism was introduced, probably at the beginning of the first century A.D. At first obscure and negligible, by the third century it had become a great dissolving influence for the traditional civilization, just as the barbarians had become a serious threat to the political and racial integrity of the empire.

Beginning from 300 A.D. eight princes of the blood of the House of Tsin started an indescribable mêlée of civil war in their mutual struggles for power. It was a signal for the barbarians that their day had come, and the Hsiung-nu of Shansi were the first to declare independence in 304 and formally occupied what had for long been virtually their territory. Other barbarians eagerly followed in their wake, and within the next century or so over a dozen ephemeral states were set up along the courses of the Yellow River. The House of Tsin crossed the Yangtze and established a new seat at Nanking, henceforth to be known in history as the Eastern Tsin dynasty (317–420).

By 376 a barbarian state comprehending the whole north had been established, known by the classical name of Ch'in, which began to consider seriously the invasion of the south and the unification of all China. But the Yangtze proved to be an impassable barrier, and the barbarian host was defeated at the River Fei, in northern Anhui, 383 A.D. The Battle of the Fei is one of the decisive struggles in history. Had the barbarians succeeded in crossing the Yangtze at a time when Chinese vitality was at a low ebb and the Chinese race had not yet taken deep roots in the new south, all China would have been lost and most probably re-barbarized, and it might have meant the end of Chinese civilization. At any rate, all future history, even if China as a cultural entity could have been preserved, would have been totally different. As it was, China had already been enough shaken, and came gradually to assume a new physiognomy. For two centuries after 383 the country was definitely divided into North and South, Chinese and Barbarian were to coalesce into a new Chinese race, and Buddism was to give a new impetus to Chinese culture. Classical China was at an end; a new cycle of Chinese history was just beginning.

III

We have agreed to call the Second Cycle that of Tartar-Buddhist China. Tartar blood, for the first time introduced at the end of the first cycle, was to become an increasingly important factor in Chinese development for the next two thousand years, when repeated waves of the northern peoples were to enter and conquer a part or the whole of China, only to be absorbed to enrich the main Chinese stream. With every wave of invasion, the Chinese of the north sent a new wave of migrants to the south, which was persistently to increase in political and cultural importance, till finally the South was to become the cultural centre of China and, today, even the political centre.

Buddhism, also introduced at the end of the first cycle, succeeded in transforming Chinese culture and giving the second Cycle a decidedly East Indian varnish, though fundamentally the Chinese have been able to preserve their spiritual identity. Whether one professes the Buddhist faith or not is of secondary importance; no Chinese of the second cycle has been able to escape entirely the influence of Buddhism in his attitude toward life.

The second cycle may be divided into five eras as follows: —

(1) The Northern and Southern Dynasties, the Sui and T'ang Dynasties, and the Five Dynasties, 383–960 A.D.;

(2) The Sung Dynasty, 960–1279 A.D.;

(3) The Yüan and Ming Dynasty, 1279–1528 A.D.;

(4) The Fall of the Ming and the Rise and Heyday of the Manchu Dynasty, 1528–1839 A.D.;

(5) The End of the Manchus and the Republic, since 1839 A.D.

It may be noted that we have not given each age a name, as in the case of the first cycle, but contented ourselves with the respective dynastic titles. Though we shall make attempts to characterize each age as we proceed, yet it can hardly be denied that politically and socially China has undergone practically no change, but has merely preserved and carried on the institutions as set up by the Ch'in and Han dynasties. Outwardly the only notable change was a panoramic succession of dynasties, which, whether Chinese or Barbarian, never deviated from the general pattern.

Really significant changes have occurred only in the cultural sphere. Politically there have only been ups and downs, while socially an even tenor has been maintained throughout. It is only during the last hundred years, under the impact of the West, that signs of a comprehensive transformation have appeared.

The six centuries after the Battle of the Fei was an age of transition and new synthesis, when Chinese and Barbarians gradually merged into one people and created a new empire and Buddhism was digested and utilized for new cultural developments. At its greatest extent, the T'ang empire was even more extensive than that of the Han. All of Manchuria, including Korea and the Amur territory, most of Mongolia, Turkestan, both Chinese and Russian, all of Tibet, and Annam all recognized the suzerainty of T'ang, while the Han emperors had never reached the Amur or Tibet. In fact, the T'ang emperor, known as Huang-ti within China, used the additional title of Heavenly Khan in dealing with the subject peoples. In this sense T'ang may be called a dual empire, composed of Chinese and Barbarians on a footing of at least nominal equality.

Buddhism reached the height of its development during the Northern and Southern Dynasties and Sui and T'ang times. Buddhist missionaries from India and Central Asia and Chinese pilgrims to the west became regular sights, and the two must have often met on midway. Buddhist sutras were extensively translated, while independent Chinese works were also being composed. Many sects were either imported or developed on Chinese soil. In so far as Buddhism was a religion, the most important sect was perhaps that of the Pure Land, which served as an unfailing spiritual refuge for the people, while all the other sects were schools of philosophy, intelligible only to scholars.

The grandeur of the Sui and T'ang lasted barely two centuries. Beginning with the middle of the eighth century the empire steadily declined, and the first decade of the tenth century again found it broken into fragments, of which the most important were the five ephemeral dynasties succeeding one another in the north. At the same time, Buddhism showed signs of decline, and the traditional Chinese culture in the form of Confucianism came forth to reassert itself. The "back to the Classics" movement, championed by Han Yü (768–824 A.D.), would do away with all foreign influences and restore the pure Chinese culture of the ancient days. A man of little originality, Han Yü was significant as the forerunner of the Neo-Confucianism that was to carry all before it in the Sung dynasty.

The Sung dynasty was an age of general stock-taking and house-cleaning. By 960 A.D. the signs of weakness had become perfectly plain. For two centuries disunion had been growing apace, and the state of union achieved after 960 was due more to a general weariness than to an active line of policy. The army, composed of hungry peasants and the social riffraff, was of little or no use even in defending the frontier, to say nothing of pushing beyond it. The finances were disorganized, with the peasants loaded with burdensome taxes and heavy corvée services. The civil service examinations, first set up by the Sui, had by this time become artificial and anachronistic, confined mostly to the Confucian Classics and producing few leaders that could understand and devise means to reform the evils of the country. In view of these considerations, it should be no matter for surprise that the Sung had never been able to gain a natural frontier. The Peiping area, lost in the period of disunion to the Khitans or Liao, could not be reconquered. The northwestern corner of the country, the northern part of Kansu and the southern part of Suiyuan, lost to the Tibetan Tanguts or Hsia, was to remain in barbarian hands throughout the age of Sung. The Sung not only failed in evening up the frontier, but, in order to purchase peace, was forced to pay a heavy yearly tribute, both in cash and silk, euphemistically known as a free gift, to the two barbarian neighbours.

Wang An-shih, the prime minister of Shen-tsung (1068–1085), was a man of deep insight and rare understanding. He clearly saw the evils besetting state and society and offered the appropriate remedies, and he would most probably have succeeded in revivifying the empire if opposition had not been too blind and selfish. As it was, the situation was hopeless, and very soon the North was once more lost to barbarians. For a century and a half the Sung managed to keep a miserable and precarious hold on South China, but ultimately all China, for the first time, was overwhelmed by barbarians, to form a part of the universal empire of the Mongols.

In the cultural sphere, however, innovations met with a better fate. The racial mind seemed to be determined to erase at least the external marks of alien influences and, in striving to revive classical tradition, succeeded in working out a synthesis of Buddhism, Taoism, and Confucianism, which, however, its exponents believed to be the original and pure system of Confucius, and which we might call Neo-Confucianism, an eclectic and synthetic product. Eclectic speculation flourished throughout the Sung era, but it is curious to note that its highest development was reached only after the loss of the North. The new philosophy diverged into two main streams, which we might call Moderate Realism and Absolute Idealism, best represented by Chu Hsi (1130–1200) and Lu Chiu-yüan (1139–1192) respectively. After 1200 there was no more development in Neo-Confucianism; all future philosophers were divided between the two schools set up by Chu and Lu. Chu, however, was gradually recognized as the orthodox master and canonized as a sage, even regarded by some as the greatest sage after Confucius.

The Mongol and Ming dynasties were an age of political catastrophe, temporary recovery, and cultural stagnation. For a full century China was at the nadir of misfortune and decline; for the first time the whole country was ruled by the foreigner. The Mongol Empire, besides, extended as far west as Eastern Europe; China formed only a part of the universal empire, albeit a huge and important part. The Mongols, again, differed from the conquerors of former ages in that they were indifferent or even hostile to Chinese culture, and had no inclination to be absorbed into the Chinese body. If anything, they would rather like to have the Chinese adopt Mongol manners and ways of life. This was perhaps the main cause why they were driven out after barely a hundred years.

Ming was the only period after T'ang when all China was unified under one native rule, with even the barbarian territories of strategic importance beyond the frontier incorporated within the empire. This outward splendour, however, had a gloomy counterpart in institutional and cultural development. The examination system was further ossified by the introduction of the so-called "Eight-legged essay," which was to bind the mind of the race with ill-understood classical allusions and stereotyped opinions. The Sung dynasty had still been able to produce such an independent and energetic spirit as Wang An-shih; the best specimen of Ming intellect could only vilify him. The absolutist system of government began to take on the most abnormal accretions. . . .

The only gleam of light in the prevailing darkness was the rise of the Cantonese and Fukienese branch of the Chinese race and its expansion overseas, thus showing that the latent vitality of the race was still capable of forward thrusts. The East Indies, known to China as the Western Seas or the South Seas, had been opened to Chinese commerce as early as the T'ang dynasty, if not earlier; and throughout Sung and Mongol times the Chinese of the south had never lost contact with the southern islands. But large-scale Chinese immigration was a Ming phenomenon, for which the impetus seems to have been given by the naval expeditions of Cheng Ho, the greatest eunuch of the dynasty and a rare specimen of his class. The Chinese of the southern coast, with some of their kinsmen already settled overseas, took the opportunity to emigrate to the islands in large numbers, sometimes amounting to thousands, including men, women, and children. Some were merchants, others worked the gold and silver mines. A few were adventurers and pirates, often defeating some native chief and carving out a kingdom for themselves. When the Spanish and Dutch arrived in the sixteenth and seventeenth centuries, some of the most stubborn resistance was led by these Chinese chiefs. This marked a new orientation in Chinese development. Historically the Chinese had been a continental people, knowing little of the sea. From the fifteenth century onwards, at least one branch of the race was being trained into seafarers.

In the realm of philosophy Yüan and the early Ming were entirely sterile. The school of Chu Hsi was triumphing over its rivals all the time, and on the establishment of the Ming dynasty it was officially recognized as the orthodox Confucianism, from which none aspiring to an official career might deviate. But around 1500 an extraordinary genius came forth to break the spell of gloom and general mediocrity. Wang Shou-jên, (1472–1528) was one of those rare combinations of talents that unaccountably appear now and then to illumine the stage of history. Statesman, soldier, strategist, scholar, man of letters, philosopher, and mystic, he was great in all these several respects, in spite of the ordeal of an orthodox training and state examinations. The last of the Neo-Confucianist philosophers and perhaps the only great man of the Ming, Wang died in 1528, a time that coincided with the decline of the dynasty and the first foreshadowings of the dissolution of the traditional order. Europeans had just arrived at the Chinese shores, and were ultimately destined to shake China to the very foundations.

The end of the Ming and the heyday of

the Manchus was an age of utter stagnation, both political and cultural. Not only were there no new stirrings of the spirit in any sphere, but no need for such stirrings was even faintly felt. Meanwhile, new menaces were looming in the horizon. For a time before the close of the sixteenth century the threat from Japan was very real, and only the unexpected death of Hideyoshi reverted the danger of a Japanese conquest of at least part of the country. Potentially, of course, the greatest danger lay in the Europeans; but, for the time being, they were still too fully occupied with the New World, India, and the East Indies to pay much attention to the outwardly imposing colossus of Eastern Asia. The people ultimately to conquer the Ming was a heretofore obscure Tungus tribe of Northern Manchuria. The Manchus, however, differed from the Mongols in that they were not antagonistic to Chinese culture. In fact, they had already started on the road of Sinicization even before the conquest of 1644, and were ultimately destined to be totally absorbed by the Chinese.

One contribution of the Manchus is of special importance. The modern provinces of Yünnan and Kueichou, though first conquered by the Han and since then never completely severed from the empire, had not yet become an integral part of cultural China even by the time of the establishment of the Manchu dynasty. The Manchus, having become Chinese themselves, were determined to civilize the aborigines that still predominated in the extreme southwest, and under Shih-tsung or Yung-cheng (1723–1735) this policy was successfully carried out. Chinese colonists were encouraged to migrate and settle in large numbers, and aborigines were persuaded to adopt Chinese ways of life. Most of the tribal chieftains were deprived of their authority, and bureaucrats directly appointed by the imperial government were despatched to rule over the new districts. Though concentrated groups of uncivilized tribesmen have remained to this day, yet Chinese culture may be said to have been firmly and irrevocably established in those far off provinces.

All further progress in the Neo-Confucianist philosophy stopped with the death of Wang Shou-jên; repetitions and readaptations of the old masters were the only product of latter-day thinkers. Intellectual effort during the Manchu dynasty was largely confined to philology and textual criticism of the classics. The only really creative work of the age was done, surreptitiously and for the most part anonymously, in the realm of fiction, which, beginning to prosper under the Mongols, reached the height of its development during the Ming and the heyday of the Manchu dynasty.

The era since the Anglo-Chinese conflict of 1839–1842 has not yet fully run its course; so it is very hard to characterize it in a satisfactory manner. From the tendencies of the last century, however, we may call it an age of general decline and disintegration and various and repeated attempts at regeneration. Both Chinese vitality and Chinese culture had been steadily waning ever since the Sung dynasty. The Manchus, after two centuries of predominance, were also weakening. There was no prospect of political and social reinvigoration, nor any sign of new stirrings of the spirit. Into the midst of such a state of torpor suddenly rushed the European, backed by a strong political machinery, an aggressive economic organization, and a vigorously expansive civilization. No wonder China was at first dumfounded, then impotently enraged, and finally collapsed. Only very recently has there been a faint prospect of recovery from the repeated blows of a century. The emperor system and the state examinations, the two main props of the traditional order, have both been abolished. All the larger cities, especially the river and sea ports, have been virtually Westernized, and the Westernization of the interior is only a matter of time. It must be perfectly plain to anybody not blind to facts that the Second

Cycle of Chinese history is drawing to a close. Just when and how the end would come, it is of course impossible to say. And after that end could we, phoenix-like, rise from the ashes and live the life of a Third Cycle? Who dare be so rash as to answer Yes or No?

IV

The method of periodization that we have adopted above is offered only tentatively. Let us see if we can find the same or similar stages of development in the other cultures. From the point of view of world history, the first cycle of China, great as it undoubtedly is, can really show little that is peculiar to itself; other peoples can boast of similar results, only somewhat differently expressed to suit different tastes. All cultures invariably start with a great number of tribes or petty states that are correlated into some sort of feudal order. Gradually they coalesce into a small number of larger and more or less national states, which for centuries lead a very animated group life among themselves, both in peace and in war. These great powers tend to annihilate one another, till finally one comes out victorious and establishes an empire coextensive with the whole cultural area. So far there has been no exception to this development; imperial unification is an unmistakable starting point, both backwards and forwards, in a comparative study of the various cultures. The events before unification are often obscure on account of the scarcity of historical material. . . . Egypt, Greece and Rome, and China are the three cases of which the events before unification are pretty well known, and from these we may say that the developments of the various cultures are quite similar, both in their nature and in the duration required. For example, the Greek states settled down about 1200 B.C., and the Roman empire was established around 100 B.C.,[1] altogether an interval of

[1] The birth of the empire is usually dated from Augustus, 31 or 30 B.C.; but, as a matter of fact, Rome had already unified the Mediterranean world by 100 B.C.

eleven hundred years. In the case of China, from P'an Keng (1300 B.C.) to the Ch'in empire (221 B.C.) is also a duration of eleven centuries. . . .

In dealing with the past, from the known we have tried to get a firmer grasp of the unknown; could we go a step further and prognosticate the fate of the future? The Western European is admittedly the most vigorous culture that is at present dominating the world situation; if possible, we should be very eager to get a glimpse of its future, which would undoubtedly involve the whole future of humanity. Unless it were to prove to be an exception, we may be pretty sure that sooner or later the Western European cultural area, which at present is about equivalent to the entire planet, would become one state, the first world empire actually to comprise the whole world. But uncertainty about the birthday of this culture makes it impossible for us to say when this important event would occur. However, we may change our method a little and make the end of the first cultural age our starting point. The first age in every culture is one of feudalistic anarchy. In China this came to an end about 770 B.C., five and a half centuries before unification. In Greece the age of the Kings was brought to a close around 650 B.C., also five hundred and fifty years before the establishment of the empire. The case of Egypt is obscure, but the exact coincidence of the classical and Chinese cultures may perhaps serve as a reliable indicator. It is generally agreed that around 1500 A.D. was the turning point between the feudal and national periods of Western European history, and, if the future should prove to be no deviation from the past, the great world empire would be established about 2050 A.D., about a century hence. The West or, in a wider sense, the World has now reached the midpoint of the era of the Contending States. The intense struggle for hegemony among a small number of world powers and the impotent position of all the other states — what is it but the middle of the fourth century B.C. of China writ large? In the case of China the most deadly wars occurred between 350 and 250 B.C., and to-day we are resigned to the fact that future wars would make the last war seem child's play, and the next century would most probably repeat in a more earnest fashion the painful history of China between 350 and 250 B.C. For such destructive eras the only way out is unification, the final and inevitable recourse of a war-weary and crestfallen world, eager for peace and rest at any price.

All that we have said above applies only to the first cycle of a culture. We have so far neglected the second cycle, because that is a phenomenon peculiar to China. No other culture has been able to start afresh after unification and the inevitable decay. . . . The Roman Empire, in its western portion, lived only for six centuries or less. The new seat set up at Constantinople, some sort of bastard of the Roman Empire, dragged on till 1453 A.D., a little over fifteen hundred years from the beginning of Mediterranean unification. China, from Ch'in Shih Huang-ti (221 B.C.) to the present, has been carrying on for over two thousand one hundred and fifty years, a record unparalleled anywhere else in the world. Mere duration by itself is already something to be reckoned with, but China has been able to accomplish the still more amazing feat of living a second life, to which no other people can show something even remotely similar. It is true that politically the second cycle is not so vigorous as the first; it has created nothing new, but has simply satisfied itself with following the pattern as set up at the end of the first. But the mere fact of an empire that has been able to hold together, with exceptions of short duration, for over two thousand years is something to be proud of; and, besides and above this, we have been able to do creative work in the cultural sphere all the time. We may be, we even ought to be, dissatisfied with many aspects of the second cycle, but we must

not forget that it is a record that only the Chinese, unique among all civilized peoples, can show.

The only case seemingly comparable with China is India. The Maurya Empire was established in 321 B.C., exactly a century before the Ch'in, and India as a cultural unit is still alive to-day. But the Asokan Empire of the third century B.C. was the first and last period of greatness in Indian history. Four hundred years after unification, around 100 A.D., India was beginning to feel the brunt of foreign invasion and conquest, and ever since seems to have been unable to free itself of alien influences. In the last fifteen hundred years there have been only two instances of Indian unification, the Mongol Empire of the sixteenth and seventeenth centuries and the British-controlled Indian Empire of today, both foreign creations against the will of India. Moreover, with the failure and virtual disappearance of Buddhism, the crystallization of the four main castes and innumerable minor divisions makes Indian society an organized social anarchy, a phenomenon that amazes and mystifies anyone who is not a Hindu. Even without foreign aggression, the internal situation alone is more than enough to render India absolutely impotent. Politically it seems impossible for India to have a second cycle. Religion and philosophy seem to be able to make a better show, but the Hindu's total lack of the historical sense has vitiated all our knowledge of Indian history; besides a vague and diffuse impression, we can see nothing like the orderly and rational development of Chinese Buddhism and Neo-Confucianism. So, even in the cultural sphere, the second cycle of China may still be said to be unique in human history.

The second cycle is our pride; but it should be also our anxiety. We have already lived longer and accomplished more than any other people; can we be sure that we are capable of an even more unprecedented wonder by creating a third cycle?

IV. MODERN LINEAL THEORIES

The Four Ages of Chinese History

MIYAZAKI ICHISADA

No European concept has affected modern periodization more than the idea of progressive history. Often the idea has meant that the periods of Chinese history were comparable to those of European. Naitō Konan, the influential Japanese historian mentioned in the Introduction, suggests the comparability in drawing a distinction between Chinese "modern" and "medieval" periods. One of his most prominent successors, Professor Miyazaki Ichisada (b. 1901), develops the idea of two additional periods. He both indicates differences from Europe and implies a general similarity of periodic development. In the essay below, written for a university textbook on Chinese history, he summarizes the salient characteristics that point to four successive and distinct ages and warns that the tenacity of traditional Chinese cultural forms makes keen observation necessary, lest significant changes go unnoticed.

Professor Miyazaki holds the chair of Oriental History in Kyoto University. His books and numerous monographs include studies of Chinese monetary, examination, official recruitment, and political systems as well as general cultural movements.

I T is no exaggeration to say that the understanding of history begins with periodization and ends with periodization. Now when it comes to making a periodization of history, what to take as the standard is a question; however, the study of history being a synthesizing science above all, its periodization must even more be built from a position that has synthesized its various phenomena. Then, when the various phenomena have been combined, the scale of that form that has been settled upon must, curiously enough, be given attention all over again.

Now, with reference to the methods of study of European history, we would propose for consideration a periodization of East Asian history divided into four ages: Age I, the establishment of an ancient empire; Age II, an aristocratic society; Age III, a period of autocratic government; and Age IV, a period of modernizing progress in East Asia.

AGE I. ESTABLISHMENT
OF AN ANCIENT EMPIRE

Ancient history can be said to be a process in which human beings who have been passing their lives in dispersion are brought gradually together. The great unification that finally occurs is the so-called ancient empire, to which the Roman Empire corresponds in European history.

Quite likely, the ancestors of mankind lived in groups like monkeys. Thereafter, as families became established, tribal communities that bound family and family evolved. These tribal communities, as they settled on the land, formed villages, the larger taking the form of cities, and what

"Tō-Ajia-shi no jidai kubun," in *Chūgoku-shi* [*Kyōdai Tōyō-shi I*] (Osaka, 1953), pp. 11–15. Translated by the editor. Used by permission of the author.

53

were city-states came into being. The city-states followed a model development in Greece and Rome, but the form of states of the Spring and Autumn period in East Asia, too, is most appropriately seen as city-states. Among these city-states, some changed gradually into territorial states. In Greek history, Athens and Sparta after the period of the Peloponnesian Wars may be regarded as having already shifted from city-states to territorial states. In East Asian history, the strong states from the latter part of the Spring and Autumn period through the Warring States period were already territorial states, while many cities that lost their political independence were embraced in the great territories.

The territorial states waged a mutual struggle for survival and, as a result of the strong gobbling up the weak, were finally annexed by the most powerful state. On the Mediterranean coasts they were conquered by the Roman Empire, and, just as that marks a high point in European history, in East Asia China was united by Ch'in, one of the seven strong states of the Warring States. Although Ch'in fell immediately, Han rose in her place and subdued not only China but also Mongolia, Manchuria, Korea, Sinkiang, Annam, and other regions and founded a great empire unprecedented in history. Therefore we treat the period from high antiquity to the Han period as Age I.

AGE II. AN ARISTOCRATIC SOCIETY

European history takes the time from the fall of the Roman Empire and the beginning of the great migrations of Germanic peoples as the medieval period. The middle ages may also be called a period of disintegration, born after the Roman Empire had broken down. In East Asian history, the period of disunion began with the Three Kingdoms when the Han Empire died and, after an apparent unification by Chin for a moment, continued from the period of anarchy of the Five Barbarians and Sixteen Kingdoms to the period of confrontation of the Northern and Southern

Dynasties. The Northern and Southern Dynasties were united by Sui, but she was destroyed in confusion immediately, and next the splendid period of T'ang arrived. The T'ang dynasty, too, however, was a period of disintegration and separatism under military groups in its latter half, and at last the period of great disintegration of the Five Dynasties arrived. The interval of about 740 years from the Three Kingdoms to the Five Dynasties, notwithstanding the great unification of Sui and T'ang, can be called a period in which, seen overall, a tendency towards separatism was strong.

In the middle ages of Europe, to be sure, the unity of the ancient empire broke down and separatist tendencies were strong, and in addition a feudal system came into being; but in China, this period gave form to a special aristocratic system without adopting a feudal system. The aristocratic families of this period, in addition to having social privileges and privately setting the people to work on the great manors they possessed, were confirmed in preferential rights attached to official positions in the court according to their family's status. Had this system advanced another step it would have become a feudal system. Why, then, did it not go that far?

Rome, the ancient empire of Europe, broke down almost completely owing to the invasions of Germanic peoples. In China, however, though from the Han dynasty damage was done in various forms by the invasions of the northern tribes, the breakdown of ancient empire did not go to completion. The [embodiment of the] ideal of the great unity was broken by the fall of the Han empire, but each of the Three Kingdoms maintained that it was the successor in Han legitimacy and wished to preserve the ancient empire. After that, north China fell into great confusion owing to the invasions of the Five Barbarians, but the Chin dynasty fled to Chiang-nan and attempted to preserve the "ancient period" on new land. The foreign tribes that invaded north China from the Mongolian region, in order to make secure their governing power, also made great efforts to re-establish the ancient empire. Because a residual force of the ancient empire remained in East Asia, regional great families were satisfied to be privileged aristocrats in the court without becoming feudal lords.

AGE III. PERIOD
OF AUTOCRATIC GOVERNMENT

A new period begins with the unification of Sung after the great disintegration of the Five Dynasties. States that appeared from this time on, not only states under Chinese but also states under foreign peoples other than Chinese, had an appearance of firmness of foundation and a lasting quality. States like those of the Liao of Mongol descent, Chin of Manchurian descent, and Hsi Hsia of Tibetan descent are examples. This bespeaks the fact that national self-consciousness had grown strong among the peoples of East Asia. It is noteworthy, moreover, that dynasties that governed China proper were Chinese and foreign one after another, as with the Sung Chinese, Yüan Mongols, Ming Chinese, and Ch'ing Manchus; but always they had a substantial, lasting quality. This was because political organization changed from Sung on, as a result of the previous aristocratic system's being broken and the ruler's autocratic power being strengthened. In fact, monarchical government is bound from the start to be autocratic, but previously that autocracy had varied according to the monarch's individual capacity. For example, Shih Huang-ti of Ch'in, Wu Ti of Han, T'ai-tsung of T'ang, and others were rulers who exercised strong autocratic government in accordance with their talents. When, however, it became the turn of their children, and they had not the capacity to exercise autocratic government, their position was usurped by others. Erhshih Huang-ti of Ch'in was murdered as the upshot of the eunuch Chao Kao's usurping the power; Kao-tsung of T'ang was manipulated according to the fancy of his Empress Wu, and in the end she arrived at the position of emperor. The form of changing the Mandate called "usurpation," in which relatives by marriage or great ministers moved over to the position of emperor in this way, had endured; but from the Sung dynasty, in which the autocratic power of the emperor was firmly established, usurpation ceased. The emperor had become bound to exercise autocratic power as a system of government, not according to his individual capacity.

Autocratic government does not mean that the arbitrary will of the emperor becomes the basis of all government. The great ministers of the central government, in addition to weighing all sorts of policies for the emperor, go on to enact them after receiving the emperor's approval. Thus only the emperor himself holds the power of handing down the final decision: however powerful the ministers, they are not given the slightest right to make decisions for the emperor. The method of operation that requires the approval of the emperor for the enactment of all kinds of policy — that is the mechanism of autocratic government.

However, with the firm establishment of the emperor's autocratic power, privileged classes like the aristocratic families did not completely disappear and the people all become equal. The emperor, in order to exercise his autocratic power and conduct government, needed a bureaucratic mechanism obedient to his orders. In order that these bureaucrats should obey the emperor, it would not do that their official positions be given them naturally according to their family's status, like the previous aristocrats. Both the qualifications for becoming a bureaucrat and the positions must be bestowed on the individual bureaucrat by grace of the emperor. What was planned to this end was the system of high-level civil service qualifying tests called the examination system. Its origins go back to the Sui dynasty, but its firm establishment and ultimate completion were from the Sung on.

The examination system comprised tests aimed at the appointment of officials, but its questions involved the explication of the old classics and classical-style composition of verse and prose. Consequently, because it required long study in order to pass the examinations, it was impossible to succeed and become an official unless one were of a leisured class. As a result, the bureaucracy was limited to the wealthy landlord class, meaning that this after all was a kind of aristocracy. In other words, the aristocratic society of Age II was not completely destroyed; its atmosphere remained in a different form in the society under autocratic government in Age III. The basic strength of tradition, the power of continuity in Chinese society, poses the danger of unwittingly overlooking even great movements in Chinese society and of thinking that the history of China was completely stagnant, without the slightest movement.

AGE IV. THE MODERNIZATION
OF EAST ASIA

When we compare the history of East Asia with the history of Europe, there is not such a great disparity between them. For trial, if we compare 18th-century Europe and China, the two are not so much apart in social organization and grade of culture. In fact, 18th-century Europe is called a period of chinoiserie, a period when China's arts and crafts won extraordinary enthusiasm and were introduced to European aristocratic society.

Europe's drawing away from East Asia and other regions, achieving a magnificent development, and forming a clearly different society were the results of the industrial revolution that began from about the middle of the 18th century. Entering the 19th century, Europe had capital that had been accumulated and huge industrial power, and she gradually colonized other regions of the world so to rule over them. Said from our side, "the ruin of Asia" had begun. China bent before England, the leading state of Europe, with the Opium War, and next Japan, too, had to sign a treaty of commerce and friendship in compliance with America's demands.

But the "ruin of Asia" was simultaneously the precursor of the "modernization of Asia." The invasion of Europe was an invasion of her industrial revolutionary culture. This new culture had the strength to destroy completely the traditional old systems of Asia and in this generated friction between eastern and western cultures; but the friction of East and West was really friction between old and new cultures. Then, as the old culture was dying, unconsciously the modernization of Asia was arranged. A string of events — Japan's Meiji Restoration, China's T'ung-chih Restoration, the 1911 Revolution, the completion of the Northern Expedition of the Nationalist government — perhaps these may not be called directly signs of the modernization of Asia, but they are certainly signposts toward modernization, casting off the old Asian culture and following in the footsteps of Europe.

Periods of Feudalism, Gentry Society, and the Formation of a Middle Class

WOLFRAM EBERHARD

The conventional threefold European division of history has often been applied to China on grounds of expediency. For Professor Wolfram Eberhard, the content of the history described in terms of social classes justifies a tripartite division, even though the character of the Chinese periods differs from the European counterparts.

In the selection that follows he examines principally the "medieval" period of Chinese history and finds it characterized by different forms of gentry society. The medieval period, however, falls within a lineal sequence which had already included an ancient feudal period and was later to enter a period of the formation of a middle class.

Wolfram Eberhard (b. 1909) has been Professor of Chinese at Ankara (1937–1948) and Professor of Sociology at the University of California since 1952.

THE necessity to divide history into periods of eras, each one characterized by the historical forces active in them, can hardly be denied any longer, even though every division somehow artificially interrupts the continuous flow of historical events. The tremendous amount of available material for the history of China also calls for periodization. The question arises: under which viewpoints and into how many great periods should the more than 3000 years of Chinese history be split? The example of European history shows that division into three periods is usually accepted as a practical expedient as well as for internal reasons inherent in the different principles of classification. In the case of China, there seems to be general consensus of opinion that the end of the Chou dynasty, i.e., roughly the year 250 B.C., marks the end of a period. Whether this first period is characterized as the "feudal period," using a sociological principle of definition, or as "decentralized monarchy," representing a political point of view, or as "Chinese monarchy" in contrast to the next period of "universal monarchy," it always remains the period of "antiquity."

Much divergence of opinion, however, exists about the next periods. While some scholars call this period "medieval" and have it ending with the T'ang dynasty or with the end of the Five Dynasties, others have it extend to the Sung or Yuan dynasties. Still others call this period "semi-feudal" or "post-feudal" and consider 1841, or 1911, or even 1949 as the end of this period. For them, there exists no "Medieval China." For the purpose of limiting and naming the post-antiquity period, practically everything depends upon the principle of definition used. A political definition would prefer a division like: (a) Period of unification (ca. 250 B.C.–220 A.D.); (b) Period of the first division into North and South (220–580); (c) Period of second unification (580–900); (d) Period of second division (900–1278); (e)

From Wolfram Eberhard, *Conquerors and Rulers: Social Forces in Medieval China* (Leiden, 1952), pp. vii–x, 1–17. Reprinted by permission of E. J. Brill, Ltd.

Period of third unification (1278–?). It remains open when the period of "modern history" is to start: with the first appearance of Western missionaries, i.e. in the late sixteenth century? The date as well as the importance of the fact remains disputable. With the first military contacts between East and West, i.e., 1842? But did this clash change so much in China? Was not the end of the Manchu dynasty, the creation of a republic much more important (i.e., 1912)? Or did we overestimate even this event so that China began to change really after 1948–9 only? But to say that China remained a "medieval state" until so recent times would certainly be regarded as an unjust value judgment.

Whatever principle is used, there will be some difficulties. For an understanding of historical processes undifferentiated periods of more than 2000 years are not practical. The erroneous impression that nothing has changed in 2000 years may arise. The Western historian did indeed not divide Western history into classical and Christian periods, the latter still continuing. For the same reason, a subdivision of some type has to be made in the Chinese history of the post-antiquity, even if the characteristics seem to be not striking. More intensive research will perhaps later provide a better usefulness of other principles for other researches. Thus we call the period of antiquity (until 250 B.C.) also "period of feudalism." Periods preceding this one have to be classified as prehistory or early history until more about the social structure of these periods is known. The next, the "medieval period," is the "period of gentry society." The term will be explained in the following chapter. Just as the term "feudal society" stems from the social structure of the ruling upper class, so the term "gentry society" designates a special social structure of the ruling group which came into origin after 250 B.C.

It cannot be denied that it was, sociologically speaking, essentially still the same group which determined the policy of China in the nineteenth century, as in the twentieth century. The definite end of this group evolves in these very years in front of our eyes. Still, there is a very great difference between the gentry of 200 A.D. and the gentry of 1900, to select any two random dates.

Sociological divisions of European history have the "modern period" begin with the end of the feudal and the beginning of the "burger" era. If this is taken to the letter, then "Modern age" started in France with the French Revolution, in Germany much later (1870 or even 1918?). But when did it begin in England? With Cromwell, or did it not yet start at all because there is still a House of Lords? But no historian or sociologist would go to such extremes and somehow all agree on a date around 1500 as the time for the beginning of a new era. For some it is the discovery of the New World, for others the Reformation, or it is the beginning of a period in which ultimately the "burger" became the leading element. If the same principle is applied to Chinese conditions, the medieval period should be terminated somewhere between the eleventh and thirteenth centuries.

Sociologically speaking, in this time the consistency of the gentry changed: before this time the leading gentry of the country consisted of cliques of different size of families of more or less equal status, the number of all gentry families of importance, i.e. those represented in the capital of the empire, not surpassing much one hundred. But from the eleventh to thirteenth century on there appears a new stratum, a kind of middle-class or "small gentry," families which are not really wealthy, but are educated. A member of the family has passed the examinations and is thus eligible for government appointment. These families usually live in the provinces, and the one outstanding man can only with difficulties manage to stay in the provincial capital or the capital of the empire. He can make a career only when he becomes subservient to one of the powerful big gentry families, who thus gains a large group of "retainers." The number of big, powerful gentry families in this period is smaller, but each family represents a power center by the great number of lesser gentry families connected with it.

At the same time, education spreads into the class of merchants and artisans. There is a general tendency of popularization: literature for the masses (novels, plays, short stories written in conversational style) begins, printed books appear on the market, the literary style even of the gentry comes under the influence of popular style. The capital is no longer the only cultural center of the empire: literary life flourishes in many cities and local "schools" develop.

The new stratum does not yet get into power. A much greater social mobility remains so far the only outlet for this group. In the course of the following centuries, this "middle class" is transformed several times, but ultimately in the nineteenth and twentieth centuries this stratum emerges as the leading social group of Modern China.

These are the reasons which determined the writer to end the period of "Medieval China" in the eleventh to thirteenth centuries. As long as more detailed sociological analyses of the crucial period do not exist, a better limitation does not seem possible.

I

The "Antiquity" of China is regarded by some as the period of feudalism, whereas others describe it as the period of a slave society. I am not going into a discussion of the different theories dealing with this special problem here, but I wish to touch upon a question of definition involved: the definition of "feudalism" or "feudal society."

*   *   *

. . . Concerning the question of the origin of feudalism, the present writer accepts the theory of A. Rüstow of the power factor, which creates feudal societies by superstratification [stratification resulting from the conquest by a group of foreigners]. Two facts should, however, be added. The first goes without saying: not every kind of superstratification results in feudalism. Secondly, in certain cases feudalism originates as a kind of "marginal social system": societies organized in the form of tribes under "chiefs," are influenced by a neighboring highly developed, often bureaucratic culture, as the neighbor who does not understand the character of "chiefdom," involuntarily invests the tribal chief with powers corresponding to a "king" or "high official." This new power, given to the "chief," in connection with "tributes" and "gifts" given to or coming from the great neighbor, changes the chief's status, so that he may become a feudal lord under certain conditions. This seems to be the case in the Yünnan society studied by Chen Han-seng and perhaps in some early societies such as I-ch'ü in Shensi in Late Chou.

To return to China: Chou society (*ca.* 1050–249 B.C.) can be called a "feudal society." For the preceding Shang period we do not yet possess enough documents to decide whether it also was feudal or not. From what is known, it seems to be possible that it was already feudal. As distinctively feudal characteristics of the Chou period I would regard the following ones: first, Chou society is the result of an *ethnic superstratification*. The Chou rulers came from Western China accompanied by a group of militarily organized tribes of non-Chinese affiliation, at least partly of Tibetan stock. They conquered and occupied Eastern China and started an expansionist, colonial activity. The Chi clan to which the leader of the tribal federation and later "king" belonged, together with the allied tribal leaders constituted the new, aristocratic upper class: the nobility. This group ruled the country, with the most important positions of power in the hand of the Chi clan. This type of superstratification has its almost exact parallels in other feudal societies. As a second feudal trait I should note that the vassals, the nobility, entered into a contract relation with the "king." Their investiture, accompanied by a written document, symbolized the beginning of this contract relation. The *contract* imposed a *mutual obligation* upon both partners: the new lord as a vassal of the king had to give military aid in case of need, had to come to court from time to time, had to make certain gifts, so-called "tributes," of an essentially noneconomic character. The king invested the vassal with a piece of land and delegated sovereign rights over this land to the vassal. Investiture with an office was also possible. In case of violation of the contract, theoretically the land or the office was to be taken away from the vassal. Otherwise the investiture was for life and normally hereditary. A third feudal trait is that the *bond* between king and vassals was an essentially *moral-religious* one: faithfulness and loyalty were the central concepts and influenced the attitude of the vassals even when the king was practically powerless. All these traits have their parallels in other feudal societies, especially in medieval Europe. In addition there are some other traits which normally accompany feudalism, but are not exclusively feudal: e.g., feudal society is normally based upon agriculture, and a natural economy; a system of communication is usually not very well developed, etc. All these features did exist in Chou China, but existed also in later periods. This Chou society had, of course, slaves, too. But there seems to be no proof that production was based upon the labor of slaves. Only if one confounds "slave" with "serf" can one speak of Chou society as a "slave society."

We are able to observe that all historic feudal societies show certain inherent factors which ultimately lead to the breakdown of the system. The result of the break-down is a new type of society, but this new society is not everywhere and not in every case the same: in Europe, the "bourgeois" society evolved, whereas in China, the result was the "gentry" society.

I am of the opinion that the two types of society are essentially different, but I would *not* describe the one as a "Western" and the other as an "Oriental" society.

II

If the concept of Chou society as a feudal, super-stratified society is correct, we should expect a deep dualism in Chou society. I believe we can see this dualism in religion, that is to say a heaven-religion of the rulers against a popular, demonistic religion, and in literature, that is to say annalistic-statistical court literature, perhaps even epic-heroic literature against folk-song, and folk-tales. Important in this connection is the dualism in law: the moral code of the nobility, later systematized by Confucius and the Confucianists, and criminal law in written form for the others, the subject class. But we can also discern a dualism in property relations. As this is a decisive point in the question of the origin of gentry society, it has to be treated here with a few more details.

When the Western conquerors were enfeoffed with land in Central or East China, they arrived there with their families, servants and bondsmen, i.e., the rest of their original tribe or military detachment. As they were foreigners in the new territory, they built a city-fortress, a "burgh" and settled as an island in the sea of natives. Thus, the typical Chinese quadrangular, regular city originated which is so similar to the Roman city and different from the typical medieval European city which was rather a center of trade than an administrative center. The new Chou territory consisted of the old Shang territory and areas either formerly independent or only loosely dependent on Shang. The population of Shang proper with its highly developed agriculture was able to support fairly large cities. But we know neither how many cities the Shang empire comprised nor how large the area was in which food supply was organized. On the other hand we know that "natives" of different stock lived in the outer parts of the Shang empire at least. We have to make a clear distinction between the Shang and the "natives."

In the period immediately after the conquest, the Chou rulers could, theoretically speaking, rely upon the production of the Shang people. It is a question whether, in view of the attitude of the Shangs, they trusted them. This question cannot be decided yet due to lack of material. In the large area of the "natives," however, the new rulers could not rely upon their production; some of these natives did not practice agriculture at all, others had "slash-and-burn" agriculture or, even if they had a more developed agriculture which produced more than what they themselves needed, they produced food the conquerors were not accustomed to eat. So, the masters had to develop other sources for their food supply. The fief-holders, i.e. the relatives of the Chou clan, Chi and its branches as well as the tribal heads of allied tribes, organized their tribesmen in semi-military cadres of eight families each. These groups left the fortress in early spring, cleared a piece of land and cultivated it for one or more seasons until the soil was exhausted, after which a new clearing was made. Ideally, these clearings should have regular form and size, as is described in the texts on the "ching-t'ien" (well-field) system. It is quite possible that these eight-family groups worked together collectively, as the texts would indicate. Thus, there was no individual property right on real estate for them. All land belonged to the "lord" who allotted parts of it for cultivation by his bondsmen. The surplus production of these units went to the city as supply for the feudal lord and his court.

*　　*　　*

A few important points have to be mentioned here. Firstly, a development which has its parallels in European feudalism, took place in China: from at least the 8th century B.C. on, the vassals behaved like their lord, the Chou king. They were still, *de jure,* his vassals, but *de facto* they acted independently. We can, therefore, in our discussion, now simply speak of "lords," meaning the Chou king as well as his *de jure* vassals, the dukes, counts, vice counts, etc., of the Chou empire. It was only logical, that some time later, such *de jure* vassals usurped the title "king," indicating the *de facto* situation.

Secondly, in China as everywhere else, there was an element of bureaucratic administration in the feudal set-up from its very beginning. As already mentioned, the supreme lord enfeoffed members of his family and other, worthy bondsmen with fiefs. The fiefholders (vassals) did the same. But the supreme lord as well as the vassals kept a certain area under direct administration. There were his palace as well as other buildings, living quarters for his personal servants, for his military guards, and his craftsmen such as carpenters, blacksmiths, sword-makers, potters, and others. From what we know of later periods, we may assume that there were even fields which produced some of the royal needs within this compound. The administration of these establishments was in the hands of a *tsai,* a kind of "major domus," and other persons with a status similar to that of a civil servant.

Soon the cities of the "lords" became centers of industrial production and constituted points of attraction for the "natives." The city became an exchange and market center. This led to the formation of a group of merchants, rising out of the ranks of the craftsmen as well as occasionally out of the natives.

The processes which went on here, are certainly highly diversified and complicated. City-dwelling noblemen and their bondsmen may have bought land from the natives in exchange for products, supplied to them by their craftsmen. They may also have taken away fields from the natives by force. Parallels, especially from Southeast Asia, indicate that intermarriages with the daughters of native chiefs often brought land into the hands of the "foreigners." Or the natives became indebted to city-people who then put their hands upon the land of the natives.

At any rate, the relation between land-owners and debtors was shaped after the model of feudal institutions, thus creating the landlord-tenant situation which differs from a feudal relation in the absence of the moral element (loyalty), the mutuality of rights and obligations, and was a more or less purely economic relation. Even if in some cases the new owners may have had the land cultivated by slaves, such relations soon also took the form of landlord-tenant relations.

It seems as if the introduction of money played an important role in these developments which led to the creation of the new class of the "gentry."

On the other hand, the lords became just as involved in these developments as the others, his bondsmen. The change on the part of the bondsmen from a paternalistic attitude towards subject sectors of the population to a more economic-minded attitude could not but also influence the lords. The tribute the natives had to pay as a symbol of their being subject to the lord soon took the character of a tax. The difference between the "tithe" of the bondsmen working on the "well-fields" and the tribute of the natives was obliterated. "Well-fields" soon disappear as separate units. The lord sent commissioners out to the natives to collect the tribute instead of receiving tribute-bringing messengers of the natives. The merchants proved to be ideal tribute-collectors. They travelled through the countryside, knew the natives, controlled them by a system of economic relations. They were even in a position to pay the tribute in advance to the lord and collect it later from the natives.

The lords regarded these collectors as their "officials" and shaped their relation towards them after the model of their household administration.

With the disappearance of the paternalistic attitude and with the growth of a more rationalistic way of thinking, interest in wars of conquest for the satisfaction of personal interests of the lords developed. This became perceivable at the time when the difference between city-people and natives in the fiefs, as a consequence of the above-described developments, was about to vanish, when assimilation was fairly advanced.

The situation was most favorable for the lord in case of conquest of non-Chou, i.e., non-Chinese territory (and later also in case of conquest of the territory belonging to another lord): he made the point that the conquest was his personal merit, and thus he felt no obligation to delegate sovereign rights in this territory to any of his bondsmen who were his soldiers. Here the lord created "military administrations," the later *hsien* or *tao*, which he had administered by appointing tax-collectors; later, often successful military leaders of lower origin. The next step in this development then was the use of "natives" as troops (foot-soldiers) of the lord, side by side with the army of bondsmen (charioteers). The use of this new type of army, over which the lord had complete and direct control, increased his power and led ultimately to the end of the armies of bondsmen, thereby to the disappearance of this whole group, and of the feudal set-up.

When the development had reached this point (historically this is around 300 B.C.), two consequences emanated: The lord, relying upon his new "popular" army could consciously fight against the remnants of the old nobility and upper class and systematically destroy it by atomizing the society. This is the step which was taken by rulers in the Near and Middle East at the end of a feudal period. In China the "Legalists" had created the ideology for such a system, and Shih-huang-ti definitely attempted to apply their ideas. One reason for the failure of this experiment is purely accidental: Shih-huang-ti died before the system had time enough to become institutionalized, and after the murder of his capable son, no successor existed able enough to continue his work. The other reason is sociological: conquest of non-

Chinese territories was possible only for the feudal lords on the periphery of China proper. These lords had their hands free and could exercise full authority in the conquered territory. All other lords, however, could conquer only land, formerly held by other feudal lords and inhabited mainly by partially assimilated bondsmen and "natives." The upper-class meanwhile had thousands of links tying them together and to merchants and other rich people in the city of the conquering lord. Moreover, here we have "landlords" owning tracts of land, rented to farmers. When at the time of conquest such a landlord and his tenants became subjects of the conquering lord, the lord naturally could not just take the land without seriously disrupting the socio-economic structure. Even as a former subject of the conquered lord, the landlord was still a power-factor; the common interest of all landlords, together with mutual relations of such landlords by marriage relations which went over frontiers, exercised pressure upon the lord in order to leave the land situation untouched. And after all, such a landlord was in every case a prospective, reliable tax-collector and administrator: he already collected his own rent from his tenants and knew his business and his farmers. So he was more efficient than a newly appointed military leader. Thus, conditions were in favor of the landlords and against a military, despotic rule. Together with the historical accident of the early death of Shih-huang-ti this prevented the formation of a pure despotism in China. We have indeed some characteristics of despotism in Ch'in and early Han time, down to the time of Emperor Wu, but meanwhile the new "gentry society" had entered the scene.

The second consequence was that the lord began to draw the landlords into his administration. This meant, sociologically and economically, the death of the old nobility and/or its transformation into landholders similar to the others. In this case it was not attempted to atomize the society. But nevertheless a differently stratified society emerged with a new ruling class, the gentry; and the ruler can no more be called "feudal lord."

III

The first typical characteristic of this "gentry society" which came into being in the third century B.C. and was firmly established in the first century B.C., is: no aristocracy or nobility exists. The upper and ruling class is a class whose power is based upon their socio-economic position. Therefore, in theory, it is an "open society": in theory everybody could enter its ranks. In Han time, we know of cases of social rise. But later on, as statistical researches made by Wittfogel and myself have proved, social rise was extremely rare. (I should like to remark here that from Sung period on conditions changed once again.) The ruling class, which I call the "gentry" in order to avoid confusion with any superficially similar class in other cultures, occupied a double key-position wherein lay the secret of its power and stability. A family, belonging to the "gentry" normally had: a) a country-home and b) a city-home. The country-home was surrounded by the property of the family, and here lived a part of the family administering the property, i.e., collecting rent from the tenants. The country-home was the economic backbone of the family. As soon as the family had enough capital it could afford to engage a tutor to give its children the education necessary to become officials in town. Tutors were not easy to find, as a man with education had better opportunities in other work than teaching. Books were the monopoly of the teachers: they knew them by heart and transmitted their knowledge to selected students only. To teach a peasant-boy would ruin their prestige; gentry families did not like to appoint a "peasant-teacher." And a peasant could hardly bring together the capital necessary to keep the tutor. The more the gentry became a class the stricter the education became. Just as the European "burger" imitated the aristocrat of earlier times, the Chinese new gentry imitated the earlier noblemen: they copied the rules of behavior for noblemen, collected in the Confucian writings. These rules now became the rules of behavior of a "gentry man" ("gentleman"). These rules were so numerous, so complicated that nobody could learn them alone without a tutor and a family background in which these rules already prevailed. These rules, the so-called "Confucianism," a system with quite a different spirit than that of Confucius, in effect, changed the gentry into a closed society, differing from the lower classes in their behavior, their language, their gestures, their morals.

The educated members of our gentry family moved into the city-home. Here they could live a life of leisure: they had the solid economic background of the country-home. So we see them as poets, painters, scholars, philosophers. Sometimes they preferred to live in the precincts of the city, in a luxurious cottage which they poetically called a "grasshut" and engaged in Taoist philosophy. This philosophical Taoism was their psychological reaction against a life within strict rules, a life in which every step was regulated, a life in the "Confucian straight-jacket," or, more often, was a temporary retirement when the political situation in the city had become unfavorable or dangerous. When things changed, our "Taoists" often returned to the city and became "Confucianists" again.

But the normal main activity of the city-branch of the gentry-family was politics. Its members tried to enter the bureaucracy as officials in the provincial or central administration, civil or military. The position of a gentry-family in the city or in the capital was fortified by marriage-alliances with other gentry-families. Thus, cliques were formed, and these cliques struggled for power. The emperor — normally of gentry origin — was the exponent of these gentry cliques. If he were intelligent and active, he could exercise a considerable power by checking one clique through another and using one against the other. If he were inactive or unwise, he could easily become a tool in the hands of one clique. Then, the development is clear: the clique tried to get rid of the other, rival cliques, and if this were achieved, the emperor was "persuaded" that abdication was the best course open to him.

The secret of the power and stability of this society lies in this double foothold: if in the struggle for power in the center one clique were exterminated, the country-branches of these families always could manage to survive. I know of no case where both branches were equally affected by a political transition. As long as the city-branch was in power, it could protect the country-branch and assist it: the young boy from the country-branch used his city connections and secured a position. He married into one of the allied families and further strengthened the power of the family. The more children the gentry-family had, the better it could fortify its position. If bandits or others attacked the country-seat of the family, the city-branch could give shelter to its relatives; it could organize military or administrative aid to get them back what they lost or more. So, this gentry class was invincible. The first and really dangerous attack against it began before our eyes, in a period when economic factors had already undermined the economic backbone of this system: the Communists with their land reform removed the city-branch. The consequences of this step are still to be seen.

The main differences between the Western "burger" society and this Chinese gentry society are as follows: a) the gentry class was economically dependent upon landed property, not upon industrial capital; b) the gentry class, comprised of landowners, scholars and politicians *in one and the same class,* normally had representatives of all three occupations *in one family,* and often one individual was at the same time scholar, politician and landlord. In the West, the scholar was always merely an appendix of the "burger" class and usually an unhappy one; the politician and official on the other hand was normally not a landlord nor had he the highest education.

The extreme stability of Chinese gentry society was the decisive factor which prevented the disintegration of Chinese civilization and militated against the success of foreign rule over China. But it also prevented change. It prevented the development of modern science — the instrument of change.

However, gentry society itself did pass through certain stages of development within limits, of course. The changes in gentry society are divided into several periods: a) period of formation (Han dynasty); b) period of assimilation of foreign, aristocratic societies (in North China, between 220–*ca.* 800 A.D.). The gentry copies some aristocratic attitudes of their nomadic rulers. Nomadic families fuse with the Chinese gentry; c) period of colonial gentry (in Central and South China, between 220–*ca.* 600 A.D.); d) period of the great gentry (*ca.* 800–*ca.* 1278): stratification within the gentry. The circle of politically leading gentry-families becomes much narrower; e) period of the formation of a middle class (*ca.* 13th century until 1949). This period falls, in our system of classification, into the "Modern" period.

The Marxian Influence

History Governed by Key Economic Areas

CH'AO-TING CHI

A debate known as the Controversy on Social History engaged Chinese intellectual circles in the second quarter of the twentieth century. By that time, a number of Chinese had taken up the view that history moved according to the control of material production by social classes, a view influenced by Marxian theory.

Ch'ao-ting Chi's contribution to periodization, reflecting that influence, sees China characterized by semi-feudalism (Oriental society) from the beginning of the Ch'in dynasty to the Opium War in the 19th century. During that long period, changeless both in the "character of society" and its "political superstructure," subordinate cycles depending upon political control of key economic areas formed historical sub-periods. Notably, Chi characterizes the sub-periods as ones of unity and peace alternating with others of division and struggle, a dichotomy recalling some traditional Chinese descriptions of periods.

Ch'ao-ting Chi (b. 1904) received the Ph.D. from Columbia University and was active in international trade and economic groups of the People's Republic in the 1950's.

B<small>Y</small> using the concept of a Key Economic Area, it is possible to analyse the function of the economic base as providing the fulcrum for the political control of subordinate economic areas in China. It thus becomes possible to study an im-

From Ch'ao-ting Chi, *Key Economic Areas in Chinese History*, pp. 2–5, 7–11. Reprinted by permission of *Pacific Affairs*.

portant aspect of Chinese economic history, to approach it from the viewpoint of political power with reference to regional relations, and to formulate it in terms of the development of agricultural productivity by irrigation and flood-control and the evolution of a system of artificial waterways, primarily for the transportation of grain tribute to the seat of government. No other method reveals so clearly the relation of political power to geographical regions in China, the recurrent dominance of one region over others, and the means by which political unity in a large territory of marked regional diversity was achieved. It is important to point out in this connection that regional economic geography has influenced the history of the peasant revolts of China (which were often the cause of a change of dynasty), both by providing a focus of rebellion and by restricting or augmenting the chances of success.

With the passing of classical feudalism in the third century B.C., China entered on a long period characterized by territorial expansion and a shifting of the economic focus, together with alternations of political control, but practically without change in either the character of society or its political superstructure. This period did not in fact end until the breaking down of Chinese isolation in the middle of the nineteenth century. It therefore includes practically the whole of Chinese history, from the beginning of the imperial or dynastic form of unification to the invasion of China by the Western Powers. Within this period, two outstanding movements can be observed. One is the alternation of unity and division effected on a more or less unvarying plane of socio-economic development, with an almost complete lack of structural change, which has often been interpreted as stagnation. The other is the southward movement of Chinese civilization from the central Yellow River basin to the Yangtze valley, which is distinctly a phenomenon of growth. In the course of the advance from the central Yellow River basin to the Yangtze valley, the relative strength and

political importance of the various regions changed progressively, with a corresponding change in the Key Economic Area as the central problem of regional control. Thus, isolating the phenomenon from the influence of invasion, peasant revolts, the development of commerce and other factors, the question of territorial expansion, together with changes in the economic and political centre of gravity, but without structural change in either social or economic forms, becomes a problem of the shifting of Key Economic Areas, the solution of which provides an important key to the understanding of Chinese history.

DEFINITION OF KEY ECONOMIC AREAS

Chinese economy throughout the long period under discussion was primarily composed of tens of thousands of more or less self-sufficient villages which were normally woven into larger groups for purposes of administration or military action. The larger unit of political administration, equivalent to the modern "province," has existed since the Han dynasty (206 B.C. to 221 A.D.). The name has been changed under different dynasties and the boundaries of individual provinces have been changed from time to time; but the provincial unit, as such, has continued almost unchanged from very early times. These provincial groupings, however, were again combined into geographical regions, according to major topographical divisions, and through economic factors. The outline of geographical regions of this kind was particularly emphasized in times of disturbance and divided rule. A comparison of maps in the disturbed years between the Ch'in (221–206 B.C.) and Han (206 B.C. to 221 A.D.) dynasties or between the Sui (589–618) and T'ang (618–907) dynasties, for instance, with maps in the equally disturbed periods of the Three Kingdoms (221–264), the Northern and Southern Dynasties (420–589) and the Five Dynasties (907–960) will bring this fact out very clearly. Commercial growth in China never reached a level which would enable it to overcome the localism and narrow exclusiveness of an agricultural economy. These regional groupings were highly self-sustaining and independent of each other, and in the absence of machine industry, modern facilities of transport and communication and an advanced economic organization, state centralization in the modern sense was impossible. In the circumstances, the unity or centralization of state power in China could only mean the control of an economic area where agricultural productivity and facilities of transport would make possible the supply of a grain tribute so predominantly superior to that of other areas that any group which controlled this area had the key to the conquest and unity of all China. It is areas of this kind which must be designated as the Key Economic Areas. . . .

ECONOMIC BASIS OF UNITY
AND DIVISION

The task of remitting annually a part of the local revenue as grain tribute was considered one of the main duties of local officials. Definite quotas were assigned to the various provinces during the Ch'ing dynasty, for instance. But in times of disturbance, only the area under the firm and direct control of the central government could be depended on for continued remittance of the tribute. Local officials or self-appointed chieftains in those areas, which the power of the central government could not easily reach, would take advantage of the disintegration of the ruling dynasty and rule these territories independently. When the areas occupied by these chieftains happened to be economically of equal strength, the objective material condition for a sort of balance of power existed, and when other factors did not upset the balance, there would be a protracted period of division. During periods of division, which inevitably involved struggle, rival rulers not infrequently resorted to the construction of public works for water-control. This competition in constructive activity, going on simultaneously with the wanton destruction common to feudal wars, generally ended with an upset of the balance and the creation of a new dominant economic area. The events during the last years of the Three Kingdoms, a classical example of division, when the complicating factor of nomadic invasion was absent, offer a noteworthy example. "From Huang Ch'u (221–226) to the Tsin dynasty (265–419), able ministers all considered the cutting of canals and storing of grain the means for military preparations."

Whenever such a dominant economic area was in existence, the chieftain who seized control of the Key Economic Area obtained a predominant material advantage over the other contending groups and could eventually put the country under one rule. With unity thus achieved, the ruling group, in order to maintain its power, generally paid special attention to the further development of the agricultural productivity and transport facilities of this Key Economic Area. The study of Chinese history from the standpoint of the Key Economic Area as a lever of control will therefore throw much light on the central question of unity and division. It will also provide a guide to the understanding of the basic objective conditions that determined the economic policy of the various dynasties in the whole period of Chinese history, from the beginning of the Ch'in dynasty in 221 B.C. to the end of the Ch'ing dynasty in 1912.

SHIFTING OF KEY ECONOMIC AREAS
IN CHINESE HISTORY

The economic history of China from 255 B.C. to 1842 A.D. (the beginning of the modern period of foreign impact), judged by this criterion, can be divided into five periods. *The first period of unity and peace* covers the Ch'in and Han dynasties (255 B.C. to 221 A.D.), with the Ching, Wei, Fen, and lower Huang Ho (Yellow River) valleys as the Key Economic Area. *The first period of division and struggle* (a most important transitional period) covers the Three Kingdoms, the Tsin dynasty and the

Southern and Northern dynasties (221–589), with Szechwan and the lower Yangtze valley, gradually developed by irrigation and flood-control, emerging as important areas of agricultural production to challenge the dominance of the Key Economic Area of the earlier period. *The second period of unity and peace* covers the Sui and T'ang dynasties (589–907), with the Yangtze valley assuming the position of a Key Economic Area and the simultaneous rapid development of Grand Canal transportation connecting the capital with the new Key Economic Area. *The second period of division and struggle* covers the Five Dynasties, the Sung dynasty and the northern dynasties of the Liao and Kin (907–1280), with additional intensive development of the Yangtze valley as the outstanding Key Economic Area in China. *The third period of unity and peace* covers the Yüan, Ming and Ch'ing dynasties (1280–1912), wtih the rulers increasingly worrying over the distance between the capital and the Key Economic Area, and repeatedly attempting to develop the Hai Ho valley (now Hopei province) into a Key Economic Area.

These five periods represent stages in the long-term change in Chinese socio-economic history, marked by the shifting of Key Economic Areas from one region to another. It goes without saying that in each period there were short intervals of social and political disturbances, frequently originating in peasant revolts, which usually resulted in the replacing of one dynasty by another, as in the downfall of the Yüan dynasty and the foundation of the Ming dynasty in 1368. Other interruptions were caused by barbarian invasions which were usually encouraged by internal economic breakdown in China such as those of the Khitan Tatars (Liao dynasty, 947–1125, the Nüchen or Juchen Tatars (Kin dynasty, 1115–1260), the Mongols (Yüan dynasty, 1280–1368) and the Manchus (1644–1912). These short cycles, however, can be better understood if they are regarded as subordinate to the long-term cycles governed by the shifting of the economic centre of gravity, which provided the setting for political and dynastic movements, whether they took the form of internal rebellion or of alien invasion.

Thus the general line of development of public works for water-control can be traced to, and understood in terms of, the necessity of holding and developing the Key Economic Area as the principle underlying the economic policy of succeeding dynasties. By clarifying the course of development of public works for water-control, the concept of the Key Economic Area illuminates a most significant feature in the historical processes of the whole semi-feudal period of Chinese history.[1]

---

[1] Dr. K. A. Wittfogel speaks of "the economic-political kernel-district of China" in his monumental work on Chinese economy and society. His contribution, however, is different from mine, although our theses are complementary to each other. He says, "The so-called 'kultural centre,' or more correctly, the economic-political kernel-district of China, was by no means situated always at the same spot. It shifted several times during the period when China was predominantly agricultural; an industrialized China would create new centers of power at new spots, because the centers of raw materials and of production of industry mostly do not coincide with the agricultural centers of production" (*Wirtschaft und Gesellschaft Chinas*, p. 273). On the basis of the shifting of the kernel-district, which he ascertained to have occurred three times, from the northwest to the northeast and then the Yangtze Valley, he formulated the conception of three stages of the development of Chinese culture. Thus his contribution lies in having brought out the fact of the changing geographical location of what he calls the kernel-districts and their relation to Chinese culture. The central idea of my work, on the other hand, is to explain the function of the Key Economic Area as an instrument for the control of subordinate areas, to indicate the manner by which the shifting of the Key Economic Area was brought about, and to provide an explanation of the economic basis underlying the alternate occurrence of unity and division in Chinese history. I am indebted to my friend Joseph Pachtman for orally translating to me part of Dr. Wittfogel's *Wirtschaft und Gesellschaft Chinas*, and to Dr. Wittfogel for providing me with the English text of the above quotation and other excerpts from his book.

The End of the Ancient Period in East Asia

MAEDA NAONORI

Maeda Naonori (1915–1949) was graduated from Tokyo University in 1939. The essay from which the following selection comes has influenced Japanese scholars inclined toward historical materialist views. In it he argues for a degree of "parallelism" in the stages of development of several East Asian societies, on the assumption that a similar course of history, marked by the existence and weight of key class relationships, may be expected everywhere. Many of the technical details of his argument have been eliminated. Most of the authorities he names are Japanese historians of China.

I

. . . The formation of an ancient unified state in China was consummated with the unification of Ch'in in the third century B.C., after the period of the Warring States. In contrast, Japan's ancient unified state was consummated at least seven or eight centuries later, in the fourth century A.D. As to the formation of ancient unified states from *Stammes-staat* in Manchuria, there were the state of the Hsien-pi in the second century A.D. in western Manchuria and Koguryō at approximately the end of the third century in eastern Manchuria. Koguryō, as is commonly known, destroyed Lo-lang Commandery in the middle of the fourth century, took possession of the northern half of Korea and, opening up land in Manchuria as well, formed an extensive ancient state. At about this time the two countries Paekche and Silla were formed in southern Korea, and in the latter half of the century troops of the ancient state of Japan split those two countries and engaged the ancient state of Koguryō in battle. Presumably these facts are well known. It is known, in short, that the formation of ancient unified states in Manchuria-Korea and Japan came seven, eight, or more centuries later than in China but that among

themselves they rose one with another in parallel.

The question here is the middle ages that extend between the time of establishment of the ancient unified states and the community of the modern period. Among scholars of this country's history it is strongly held that the Japanese middle ages, which are thought of in association with the concept of a middle age founded on European history, began from about the twelfth or thirteenth century. Among scholars of Korean history, however, the prevalent view is that the middle ages in this sense began in the tenth century with the establishment of the Koryō kingdom or in the seventh century with the unification of the peninsula by Silla. In contrast to the time of formation of the ancient unified states, the time of the middle ages of Korea is fixed from three to six centuries earlier than Japan.

Whether it is possible to use the term middle ages with regard to China in the world-historical sense has become a special question requiring complicated considerations, difficult to review in detail here. I would, however, introduce two or three forceful opinions that establish a world-historical middle age also in China. One is the view, advanced by Dr. Naitō Konan

From Suzuki Shun and Nishijima Sadao, ed., *Chūgoku-shi no jidai kubun* (Tokyo, 1957), pp. 349–367. Translated by the editor. Used by permission of University of Tokyo Press.

and followed and advocated by Orientalists of Kyoto University, . . . that makes the period from the Five Barbarians and Sixteen Kingdoms to the middle of T'ang a middle age. Dr. Naitō, to be precise, delimited the true middle ages in that way, but his successors differ somewhat on the early and late limits while taking his period as the heart of the matter. Professor Miyazaki [Ichisada], for example, has put the opening of the middle ages at Ts'ao Ts'ao's Wei dynasty. At one time in the discussion of stages of development of Chinese history, a splendid debate ran in the *Readers' Miscellany* [*Tu-shu ts'a-chih*] as the Controversy on Social History. Among the various theories, the one advocated second by T'ao Hsi-sheng, putting the middle ages from the period of the Three Kingdoms to the end of T'ang, was practically the same as that of the Kyoto school. Again, the opinion of Soviet academic circles, which have begun the middle period of China from the Three Kingdoms, may be said to be close to this.

In contrast, there is a view that the middle ages began from the Ch'in dynasty or the middle of the Spring and Autumn period. . . . [Among others], a way of thinking that takes the period of political feudalism that existed in Chou dynasty China and makes it the same in essence as the medieval feudal system of Europe continues to have elemental strength among Chinese historians. This is not advanced solely by those of an anti-materialist historical outlook; even among those who hold to a materialist view, . . . there are some who advocate it.

If, proceeding from such viewpoints as those just cited, a world-historical middle age, or even a middle age common to the East Asian world alone, could be determined in East Asia, approximately a thousand years' difference in social development would exist between China and Japan even according to the Kyoto school, which finds the middle age latest, since in China the middle age would begin in about the third century. In the other views, the gap would

become from one thousand several hundred years to two thousand years or more. In short, it appears that Japan accomplished in mere centuries, from about the thirteenth, a development through and beyond the middle ages, which in China lasted from one thousand to two thousand years. Among Japan, China, and Korea, civilized regions in mutual contact from ancient times, could such a thing really have happened? In a Korean society that ran rather parallel in its time of establishment of an ancient state, did a world-historical middle age come that much sooner than in Japan? Again, if China's world-historical middle age be sought in the periods in which it has, Japan and Korea would have received the culture of China's middle age in their ancient period. Even from the point of view of the cultural historians who look upon East Asia as a unified cultural sphere, would that be true? After all, if we give no thought to the progression of years of world history in China, Japan, and Korea or to the periodization of the common social history of East Asia, are we likely to determine their respective aspects that are essentially different and unconnected?

II

Quite recently Associate Professor Utsunomiya Kiyoyoshi [b. 1905] published in the journal *Tōkō* (No. 2) an essay called "The Domain of Oriental Medieval History." Although what he calls the Orient is equivalent to what I call the East Asian world, it has not been made clear here how the medieval history of China that he has studied is to be applied also to Japan and Korea. Accordingly, there is no other way to accept it than as "The Domain of Chinese Medieval History." His middle ages seem to be based on the insight of Dr. Naitō, but a degree of difference appears. Dr. Naitō did not think of the middle ages in the same way as the middle ages of European history. Since Mr. Utsunomiya, however, makes this period one of a "self-supporting, self-sufficient man-rial economy," it would seem, though he asserts a lack of connection with Occidental history, that the middle ages of Western Europe are indeed on his mind. To be sure, this does not begin only with him; many of the Kyoto school are the same. . . .

Truly Dr. Naitō was a rarity among scholars of the world in his penetration of Chinese history. His views of the differences in Chinese society before and after the end of T'ang . . . were brilliant theses even among men of learning. . . . His idea that the modern period begins with the Sung, the late T'ang and Five Dynasties being a transition period, is fully proven. However, on the question in what does his middle age, which begins with the Five Barbarians and Sixteen Kingdoms after a transition period from the latter half of Latter Han to Western Chin, differ from the ancient period before it, a detailed opinion has not been published. Almost nothing has been advanced in regard, especially, to changes in society. . . . Was it not Dr. Naitō's view that the social differences . . . appeared not so striking, not so fundamental, as those in the period of which late T'ang was the point of divergence? As the names high antiquity and middle antiquity show, was it not felt that as between the modern age and the ancient period, middle antiquity or the middle age resembled the ancient period?

If we ask in what lay the "internally-contained" differences between the ancient period and middle age spoken of by Mr. Utsunomiya, who stresses them more than Dr. Naitō, the former raises the point that in contrast to the totally organized Ch'in and Han period, which was governmental, the middle age was atomistic. As instances of the atomistic, he first cites the strengthening of the independent existence of great families socially and economically, and again, "the founding of independent states." That, however, is hard to see as a fundamental difference between the ancient period and the middle age. It may be called, obviously, a phenomenon of a time of fighting. Even in what he calls the ancient period, the Warring States period, this "independent existence" may be seen. On the other hand, in the middle age, in the Sui-T'ang period, this independent existence of powerful families was, to the contrary, weakened. Since citing this independent existence will not do to prove an atomistic nature in the Sui-T'ang period, he refers instead to the examination system for the appointment of officials and the Twice-a-Year Tax law. These very things, however, are leading phenomena of the modern age spoken of by Dr. Naitō, not special characteristics of the middle age of the Kyoto school. Again, with reference to the self-contained, self-sufficient manorial economies of the Six Dynasties period, he has written that they disappeared under the imperial unification of the Sui-T'ang period. On examination it appears that the manorial economy itself has not hitherto been a special characteristic through the entire middle age expressed by the Kyoto school. . . .

III

It must be said that after Dr. Naitō, the most outstanding on medieval theses in the Kyoto school has been, after all, Professor Miyazaki. According to him the middle age appears to be from Ts'ao Ts'ao [155–220] to late T'ang. As its characteristics he has raised in the works cited above generally three points in comparison to the modern age. They are 1) in the middle age the principle of all the people of the country as soldiers obtained; 2) the leading stratum of society were bureaucratic great families; 3) the great families had their farming done by bound farmers. As to contrasting characteristics of the ancient period up to the Ch'in-Han period, aside from a system of state ownership of land, they are not clear. . . . Let us, then, compare the above three points that constitute the special features of the so-called middle age with the ancient period as he speaks of it. As a "rule," did not the "principle of all the people of the country as soldiers" stated by him apply in Ch'in-Han times as well? Were the garrison-troop system of Western Wei and later and the "conscript" system of Han . . . fundamentally different? On this point alone it is conceivable that there was no distinction between the ancient period and the middle age. Moreover, in the period of Wei, Chin, and the Northern and Southern Dynasties, powerful families maintained private troops, but those troops were slaves or half-slaves. The lack of a feudalistic lord-vassal relationship bespeaks the fact that this period was ancient. Next, the great families. The professor says, "Great families were transformed from feudalistic families at the time of the change from Ch'in to Han into wealthy, landholding, great families. They . . . gradually changed into bureaucratic great families but in Wang Mang's time [pp. 9–23] had not yet become purely bureaucratic." Therefore the difference between medieval and ancient great families lay only in whether or not they were bureaucratic; but even though we take the medieval great families to be bureaucratic, in being wealthy, landlord families they may not have differed from the Han dynasty. . . .

Next, the question of bound peasants. Because it is an important proposal, however, I should like first to make clear the system of national ownership of land, a system that also may be considered to be at the heart of his thesis of ancient period and middle age. In his famous essay, "On the Household Tax Ordinance of Chin Wu Ti," (Tōa keizai kenkyū 19), he stated, "The [Chin taxable-fields law] absorbed the military fields of Wei and became the model for land laws afterwards until Sui and T'ang. This very Wei-Chin land law was a great, epoch-making event that separated the middle age from the ancient period." In [another study], he said, "The [Wei military fields] were the fountainhead of the system of national land-ownership." In the Han period, however, the so-called name fields occupied by the people were not the only lands; it goes

without saying that lands directly administered by the state did not begin with Ts'ao Ts'ao's military fields. In the Han period were public fields and military fields, and the state administered them directly, using them to aid finances. Apparently Professor Miyazaki thought that the public and military fields were so small that they constituted no question, but when we see that public fields existed in commanderies and fiefs of the whole country and repeatedly gave loans or gifts to relieve the poor, were they not of great area? Among the military fields, many were public fields cultivated by troops on the frontiers, but in time of fighting these seem to have been administered as public fields of the interior. Presumably the reason given for the change of the land tax at the beginning of Latter Han from one part in ten back to the old rate of one part in thirty — "Now the grains of the soldiers' fields have piled up in surplus" (Hou Han shu, Kuang-wu chi) — indicates that this was applied even to the lands of the military fields and that the area of the public fields was great. Probably this kind of thing occurred on a greater scale among the Wei military fields, but it is well to notice that it is patterned after the Han dynasty public and military fields. If we do, is it not difficult to agree that those of Wei and Chin were the source of the system of national ownership of land? If we see that the occupied fields, public fields, and taxable fields of the southern of the Northern and Southern Dynasties approached the style of the Han period, it would seem that a single strand ran through the land systems, passed on to the Southern dynasties from the Han through the Wei and Chin. On this point the equal-field laws of the Northern dynasties, though originally founded on the previous public, military, and taxable fields, represent a kind of departure. That, surely, is an effect of the northern tribes who were the conquering peoples. Among the northern tribes a strong public ownership of land is maintained even now, but in the ancient period it was even more so. The promulgation of equal-fields systems and the prominence given national land-ownership as the principal system were likely caused by northern tribes becoming the governors. If, like the Professor, we make "the system of national ownership of land" the point of difference between ancient period and middle age, do we not have features of the ancient period continuing in the center of China until the Sui dynasty and in the north until Western Chin? In other words, I think that the "system of national ownership of land" that comprised the equal-field system was a feature of the ancient period. Be that as it may, let us turn to the question of peasants.

IV

Professor Miyazaki has not stated clearly what the state of peasants was in the ancient period, but . . . cultivators of the Former Han seem to be regarded as slaves. He also says that from the Latter Han, the local shrine system of farm villages having been destroyed and the regions made the private property of a minority of great families, the peasants became serfs of the great families. In essence, he takes it that the great families of Wei, Chin, and the Northern and Southern dynasties, for whom farming was primary, employed serfs. First let us see whether the cultivators, the basis of the great land-holding families, were, as he says, divided before and after Latter Han into serfs and slaves. Dr. Niida Noboru [b. 1904], who has said in his *History of Chinese Law Relating to Status* that in the Ch'in-Han period slaves "rose to an especially huge number," has also cited in that work numerous evidences of them engaged in farming as productive slaves. The contention of Mr. Moritani Katsumi [b. 1904] and Wittfogel that Han slaves were nonproductive is no more than empty theory. In what the historical materials show, slaves were also used extensively for farming in the Wei, Chin, and Northern and Southern dynasties period. On the other hand, it is also a fact

that large landowners had farming done by serfs. . . .

Dr. Niida in the book cited above has offered as evidence that agricultural slaves existed even in the Wei of the Six Dynasties the phrase in the *History of the Wei*, "For methods of farming ask the field slaves." As he has also shown, the same words appear in the biography of Shen Ch'ing in the *History of the Sung* [*Sung shu*]: "Administering a country is like administering a family; for farming you should ask the slaves, for weaving the house-girls." (*Sung shu* 77 Nan shih 37) That this was said through the Northern and Southern dynasties shows that in this period slave cultivation was extremely common. In fact, Dr. Niida has cited from the biography of Su Ta-yüan in the *History of the Chou* [*Chou shu*] an instance in which the proprietor of a mere two *ch'ing*[1] of fields in the Chou dynasty, the last of the Six Dynasties, has his land worked by four slaves. To mention one of the many other instances of slave cultivation by great landholders in the Wei, Chin, and Northern and Southern dynasties period, even the famous poet of the farm, T'ao Yüan-ming [365–427], has written in "The Return" that when he went back to the farm that was about to be overrun with weeds, "The slaves greeted me." From this we know that though he may have worked the land himself at times, he also used slaves. . . .

It would be hard to arrive at [a] judgment for the period of the Northern and Southern Dynasties; but, among the Southern dynasties, for example, we might cite the notation from the biography of P'ei Chih-heng in the *History of the Liang* [*Liang shu*]: "He assigned several hundred slaves to Shao Pond and set out great fields and quarters, achieving a rich store." (*Liang shu* 28) It would probably be hard to refute even the assertion that slaves played a large part on the great landhold-

[1] For general purposes, one *ch'ing* is considered to be about 15.13 acres in modern times. [Editor's note]

ings. In the Northern dynasties also, the assignment of land to slaves as well as the people upon the enacting of the equal-field system, together with being a step in the maintenance of great landholdings, suggested that those lands were mainly worked by slaves. In fact, in the *Account of Customs of Kuantung,* which has conveyed best the actual conditions under the equal-field system, it says, "Those who occupied broad lands, following orders, their slaves asked for fields." We can infer that those who occupied broad lands, that is, the great landholders, had their lands worked by slaves. My teacher, the late Dr. Katō Shigeru [1880–1946], at the end of years of study asserted, "Certainly in the Warring States, Ch'in, and Han; and up to the end of the Northern and Southern Dynasties, tenants were not so very numerous. The great acreage of the great official families was farmed mainly by slaves. About the time of the disruption of the equal-field system, however, the use of slaves in farming declined and the use of tenants became prevalent." (*Shina keizaishi gaisetsu*) I think that is an incontrovertible thesis. That great families in the period under the equal-field system of Sui and T'ang used many slaves is evident in the official histories, and there are good examples of the great landholders' use of slaves in farming in the house registers discovered at Tun-huang. One of them is the house register of So Ssu-li, head of family, 969. Since this comprises five good people and four slaves, the two *ch'ing* and forty-three *mou*[2] of fields it receives are accounted for, as Wang Kuo-wei [Chinese historian, 1877–1927] says, by the cultivation of them by the male slaves. Beyond revealing the existence in China of slaves, an outcaste people distinct from serfs, this provides nothing, to say the least, on which to decide that in what is called by a gentleman like Professor Miyazaki the middle age, great families had farming done by

[2] For general purposes, one *mou* is considered to be about 0.15 acres in modern times. [Editor's note]

serfs. We may not say that in Former Han and the Wei, Chin, and Northern and Southern Dynasties, there was a difference of slave and serf among the principal cultivators of the great landholdings. Even from this viewpoint I find not the slightest obstacle to seeing the Professor's ancient period and middle age as one ancient period. Furthermore, concerning the estimable opinion that the private sequestering of regions by great families began from the Latter Han, I should like to think, from the prevalence of concentration of land to be discussed next, that it was already so in the Former Han.

v

As said so far, it is almost difficult to distinguish the middle age of the Kyoto school from what it calls the ancient period. Next, let us consider the view that puts the middle age from Ch'in and Han or from the middle of the Spring and Autumn period. In fact, there seem to be men of this view even in Kyoto, but for now we leave that unexplained. Because Messrs. Sano Manabu [1892–1953] and Kuo Mo-jo, who hold this view, are both proponents of an historical-materialist outlook, the assertion of their thesis of the middle age is grounded on the view that a period of manorial economy or agricultural slave system began from this time. Because Mr. Kuo and others are bound, as the words "period of manorial economy" show, to admit that large landholdings were decisive, I think that their thesis of the middle age is not established, on the grounds, as has already been argued, that farming of large landholdings acquired its main form through slaves in the Ch'in and Han periods. The most difficult question to answer is whether large landholdings were decisive in the Ch'in-Han period. I can make no clear assertion about this, but it is presumably a fact that, except the directly administered state lands, the occupancy of great lands was at a peak. We can infer what has been said above from, for example, such statements as that in Wang Mang's ordinances

— "Ch'in being without the Way it destroyed the systems of the sages and abolished the well-fields, bringing it about that concentrations of land arose and the poor were born; the strong marked off fields by the thousands and the weak had not room to stand an awl in" — or in Tung Chungshu's [179? B.C.–104?] memorial — "For the rich the field dividers stretch one after another; for the poor there is not ground to stand an awl in" (*Han shu,* Shih-huo chih) — though these may be exaggerated. . . .

I think that the use mainly of slaves for farming the great occupied lands that were so prevalent, viewed from the standpoint of the ancient period in world history, was a phenomenon of the ancient period. Of course I am neither denying the existence of self-managing peasants and serfs from the Ch'in-Han period on nor maintaining that their numbers were smaller than those of the farming slaves. If the idea of Ch'in-Han as an ancient period be established in the manner of the Kyoto school, I think that we ought to take the time through Wei, Chin, and the Northern and Southern Dynasties up to the middle of T'ang as ancient. This period, in that powerful families that were the forces propelling history administered great holdings of land and based their operation mainly on the labor of slaves, has the feel of the ancient period. In other words, in contrast to the China farmed by self-managing peasants and tenants from the end of T'ang into Sung and beyond, prior to that time, as far back as the Warring States period, a large part of the farming people were slaves and half-slave serfs. In that, I think, is the nature of the ancient period. . . .

The basic force that caused the disruption of the equal-field system and at about the same time a shift from slaves to the use of tenants for the farming of the great landholders lay in the development of China's productive power. . . . There was a development of productivity of double or more. Probably this proceeded from the effect of advances in techniques of irrigated agriculture over the dry fields of the Han dynasty, but the regions of this irrigation agriculture expanded, the center of gravity of the productivity of the empire shifted to those regions, and, when in addition double cropping spread in the dry field zone, Chinese society changed. The period before the advent of this change I should like to regard as the ancient period; but in terms of the antiquity of Chinese history, it amounts to a very long continuous period. I should like to divide it into four eras. One would be what Dr. Naitō called the era of middle antiquity, one would be the era from the Warring States to the Latter Han, and now two would be the clan period and the ancient feudal period; but where to end the ancient feudal period I do not yet know. The ancient feudal period was one in which feudalism operated politically but, as Tu Yu [735–812], editor of the *T'ung tien* said, "The nobles received not exclusive fiefs, the gentry received not exclusive lands. . . ."

Problems in the Communist Periodization
of Chinese History

CHIEN PO-TSAN

In the following text of an address to Japanese historians, Chien Po-tsan (b. 1898) states the doctrinal premises within which Chinese Communist periodization works and indicates the phases of history regarded as crucial. Chinese scholars under the Communist authority have narrowed the questions of periodization to fit a single universalistic course of history. They are said to agree unanimously that the Chinese passed through the same sequence of historical periods as everyone else, granting certain variations in the manifestation of the periods, especially in modern times. With the order and nature of the periods fixed, what remains is to demonstrate when and how the periods succeeded one another.

Chien Po-tsan was active in the Kuomintang during the 1920's and early 1930's. By 1955 he was a member of the Academy of Sciences in Peking. In the decade of the fifties he was also a member of a number of missions abroad, during one of which he gave the following lecture.

I

Dear friends, I am very elated to have the opportunity to come visit the great fatherland of you our neighbors and to meet Japanese historians during the visit. And now please permit me, representing the historians of New China, to express our sincere, intimate, brotherly feelings of general friendship towards you.

In order to further our mutual understanding in the field of historical study, I should like now to introduce simply the state of the historical science of New China in the several years since the liberation.

In the field of Chinese historical studies in the several years since liberation, many new problems have been introduced. I should like now to speak to only the most important among them, that is, the problem of the periodization of Chinese history.

The true picture is one clearly known by Japanese historians: historians in

China's past in respect of the periods of Chinese history have generally all advanced it and interrupted it by dynasties. In other words, they have made rules for periodizing history according to the external phenomena of politics. Clearly, to use the external phenomena of politics to divide history periodically makes it impossible to grasp the internal reality of history. In order to explain exactly the development of Chinese history, we think that we must study the history of the development of productive power of the respective periods of Chinese history and the changes in the relationships of production brought about by the development of productive power — these most fundamental questions. Only in this way can we then discover the nature of the objective laws of the course of history behind the external political phenomena; only then can we sympathetically and wholly set out and explain the complete course of the develop-

"Kuan-yü Chung-kuo li shih fen-ch'i ti wen-t'i," *Tōyōshi kenkyū* XIV: 4 (1956), pp. 93–102. A Japanese transcript is in Suzuki and Nishijima, *Chūgoku no jidai kubun*, pp. 61–76. Translated by the editor. Used by permission of the Toyoshi-Kenkyu-Kai.

ment of Chinese history. To this end, historians of New China have very spontaneously raised the question of the nature of society in the respective periods of Chinese history; and have raised the question of the periodization of Chinese history as the nature of society has come to be debated.

II

First to discuss the question of the periodization of the Chinese ancient period.

In the field of study of the history of the Chinese ancient period, China's historians affirm that the various forms and individual historical stages in the development of society as experienced by mankind have been experienced in the same way in China. In China have been experienced the primitive communal system, slave system, and feudal system; and, moreover, before the capitalism of foreign countries invaded China, even spontaneously generated buds of the elements of capitalism were in the mercantile economy of the feudal society of China. Even if there had been no invasion of the capitalism of foreign countries, China's history could have slowly moved towards a capitalistic society. Therefore, the questions that have loomed large in the debate on the problem of the periodization of the history of China's ancient period are not the questions whether this or that historical form or historical stage existed in Chinese history; they are questions of the beginning and ending of these historical forms or historical stages. Most important among these is the question of the time and steps of the transition from slave system to feudal system.

The question of the time and steps of the transition from slave system to feudal system is not at all a new one for China's progressive historians to discuss; it is a question raised twenty-odd years ago, and a great many Japanese historians in the past have also contributed to this debate and expressed their views. But straight to the present, various different viewpoints still exist on this question and a solution has still not been achieved. To solve this question we still await continuing and deepened study and debate.

In this question the focal point of dispute is whether the society of Western Chou from the 11th century B.C. to the 8th century was a feudal society or slave society. One position regards the slave system as already completed in the Yin dynasty and the Western Chou as already the first phase of feudal society. Another position argues that Western Chou was still a slave society and takes the Spring and Autumn and Warring States period as the time of transition from slave system to feudal system. But neither of these two approaches has yet been generally accepted. At present, China's historians are at work on deep studies for advancement of Yin and Chou history and are continuing to debate the question.

The historians who maintain that Western Chou was a slave society assert that in Western Chou iron tools had not yet appeared. Therefore it could not introduce enormous changes in productive power and consequently could not produce a feudal society. But the historians who maintain that Western Chou was a feudal society then assert that this is simply a theory of instruments. To decide whether a society is slave or feudal lies not only in whether it has iron, it is necessary at the same time to give attention to changes in the relations of production. That is because similar tools of production can make for two basically different natures of society.

The historians who maintain that Western Chou was a slave system assert that the "Six clans of the people of Yin," "Seven clans of the people of Yin," and "Nine clans of the surname Huai," as recorded in *Tso chuan*, Ting kung 4th year, were all slaves and take these as one evidence that Western Chou was a slave society. The historians who maintain that Western Chou was a feudal society, on the other hand, cite notices in *Tso chuan*,

Yin kung 6th year, to assert that "the nine clans by surname" were peasants, not slaves. (Yin kung 6th year: "The nine original clan-branches of I, with the *representatives of* the five ministers *of the time of Yin,* and Chia-fu, son of Ch'ing-fu, went to meet the Marquis of Chin in Sui, and escorted him back to Go." [Legge translation.]

Historians who maintain that Western Chou was a slave system cite the speech of the Duke of Chou to the remnants of the Yin people in the *Books of Chou,* To-fang p'ien: "You now still dwell in your dwellings and cultivate your fields." They assert that these fields and dwellings were not owned by slaves, they were only turned over to them to use. Historians who maintain that Western Chou was a feudal system do not agree with this approach. They assert that slaves fundamentally could not continue to retain their own fields and dwellings and that the two sections "Numerous Regions [To-fang]" and "Numerous Officers [To-shih]" were addressed principally to the aristocratic slave-owners of the defeated state of Yin-Shang.

Historians who maintain that Western Chou was a feudal society cite from the *Book of Songs,* Ta t'ien: "May it rain first on our public fields,/ And then come to our private!" and from the *Songs,* Ch'en kung: "Order all our men/ To be provided with their spades and hoes:/ Anon we shall see the sickles at work." They assert that the producers of Western Chou already had their own tools of labor and in practice the land assigned to them, and that part of the time they attended to production on the land of their own use and part of the time on the land of their lord. This form of exploitation of the direct producers was already a form of exploitation of a feudal society. Historians who maintain that Western Chou was a slave society then assert that the private fields referred to in "May it rain first on our public fields,/ And then come to our private," were the private fields of the field officials of the old songs. As to the two

lines, "Order all our men/ To be provided with their spades and hoes," that is the wish of the King of the country expressed to the field-officials: "We call upon the farmers to arrange well the farm tools administered by the field officials."

Historians who maintain that Western Chou was a feudal society cite the fact that among 150 or 160 Western Chou tombs that archaeological workers have dug, only in three tombs were six persons buried with the dead. They take this as proof that Shang and Chou had different superstructures and therefore had different economic foundations. Historians who maintain that Western Chou was a slave society then assert that the Shang tombs of Anyang were the tombs of Shang dynasty emperors and kings but the Chou tombs mentioned above were not tombs of Chou dynasty emperors or kings. The statuses being different, they are incomparable.

Historians who maintain that Western Chou was a slave society assert that the system of clan lineage laws was really a patriarchal system, the remnant of a clan system. Historians who maintain that Western Chou was a feudal society then assert that this system was inseparable from feudal relations of production and was the superstructure of a feudal society.

Summing up this question, opinions are very diverse. Whether Western Chou was after all a slave society or feudal society is still in the stage of scientific debate. Only when we have taken hold of more historical data will we be able to decide basically whether the feudal relations of production of Western Chou already occupied a dominant position or were still one formation within a slave society. Also, only then will we be able to decide whether the revolution between Yin and Chou only shook the foundations of the slave system a bit or had decisive significance for the establishment of the feudal system. But the historical materials relating to Western Chou and presently held by us, including objects we have newly discovered in the earth at Anyang, Hui-hsien, Loyang, Cheng-chou, and other places in the years since liberation, are still not enough.

As is well known by Japanese historians, the historical materials we have on Western Chou are in part China's old scriptural documents like the *Book of Changes, Book of History, Book of Songs,* etc., in another part inscriptions on Chou dynasty bronzes, and in still another part unearthed Chou dynasty objects. Among these materials the principal sources are the materials in the old classical documents, especially the *Book of Songs*.

However, regarding the nature of the period of the songs in the *Book of Songs* there are different opinions; regarding the interpretation of the songs there are even different views for single words. Moreover, even in regard to a great many of the nouns most important socio-economically, such as "farming-man (*neng-fu*)," "one appended-to-farming (*li-neng*)," "blackhaired-people (*li-min*)," and others, whether after all their real significance indicates slaves, serfs, or even free men, Chinese historians have not yet a consensus. Many other nouns, like public field (*kung-t'ien*) and private field (*ssu-t'ien*), are also like this. Therefore, for the solution of these questions we await, on the one hand, the discovery of new historical materials in the earth and, on the other, still more profound study of the old classical documents.

III

In the field of the study of the history of the Chinese ancient period, aside from the debate on the nature of Western Chou Society, still other historians maintain that Ch'in and Han were still slave societies and regard the disintegration of the Han empire, in which had occurred the Yellow Turban rising and later the nomadic peoples' invasions of China, as the beginning of feudal annexation and a sign that feudal relations of production had won a victory. They assert that the transition from slave system to feudal system was in the second and third centuries of the common era.

Those who maintain this assert that in the Ch'in-Han period national and private slaves were very numerous and that great numbers of slaves were used in handicrafts, mining, salt deposits, trade, construction, husbandry, and transportation. They can also find evidence of the use of slaves in agriculture, but they acknowledge that what formed the foundation of agricultural production was peasants (*neng-min*), not slaves. They assert that the peasants mentioned in the *Records of the Grand Historian, History of the Han Dynasty,* and *History of the Latter Han Dynasty* were not peasants in a feudal society but members of communes in a slave society. Therefore the discussions there of peasants as slaves did not spring from feudal exploitation but came as a result of the slave system's smashing the communes. Consequently they explain all the orders of the rulers of the two Hans to free slaves and prohibit wanton killing of them, including Wang Mang's reforms, as the slave masters' efforts to soften the resistance of the slaves.

Historians who maintain that Ch'in-Han was a feudal society assert that from the Warring States period on, land had already passed into private property of landlords and by the Ch'in dynasty, "The fields of the rich joined their dividers one after another; the poor had not land to stand an awl in." By the period of the two Hans, very many great landlords used the poor for hired farming and practised feudal exploitation grandly. Therefore the principal mode of production of the Ch'in-Han period was already a feudal system, not a slave system. Those who maintain this also recognize the existence in the Ch'in dynasty and the era of the two Hans of a large quantity of public and private slaves, but they assert that the slaves of this period were already different from the slaves of a slave society and existed only as remnants of the slave system within the feudal society. Moreover, the proportion of the number of slaves in the total population figures of that time was extremely small. At the same time, the principal source of slaves was not the same as the slaves of a slave society; it was foreigners captured in war or the poor of their own people. These poor people were not members of communes, they were peasants who had to pay one-half the produce of their own land as tax to feudal landlords. Their transformation into slaves was not the result of the smashing of the communes, it was that of bankrupt peasants driven off the land by the feudal landlord class. Historians who maintain that Ch'in-Han was a feudal society also acknowledge that in the Ch'in-Han era a few slaves were still used in handicrafts, trade, mining, salt deposits, and transportation, but the great majority of slaves was put to unproductive uses, and the bands of public slaves imposed a heavy burden on the producers. As to those used in agricultural production, they were even fewer. But the principal production of a feudal society, especially in our China, is in fact agriculture. Those principally responsible for agricultural production at that time were peasants. And the peasants of that time were no longer slaves, because their masters could no longer freely kill them. Nor were they members of communes, because between them and the landholders there were already relations of personal bonds of a feudal nature. Other than this, they also point out, the law of the Ch'in-Han period, granting that law serves its economic foundations, was no longer in the service of a slave system. To the contrary, it was something that opened the way for the development of feudalism a step further. Last, they also bring evidence of their own assertion from the forms of thought, saying, "In the first years of Western Han the revering of the theories of Taoism was in reality the thought of an independent, self-sufficient small landlord class. By the time of Han Wu Ti, the honoring of Confucius and respect for the Six Classics carried the complete thought-patterns of a large landlord class into the temples. Society had not only been changed in its foundations, everything connected with the superstruc-

ture changed its appearance completely" (Kuo Mo-jo's words).

In regard to this extraordinarily important question of the decline in China of the slave system and rise of the feudal system, although varied opinions such as these exist, opinion is unanimous on the following problems: that China passed through a period of slave society; that feudalistic relations of production then took shape very early in China; that China was first among societies of the ancient period to cast off the chains of the slave system; but that for a very long period after casting off the slave system, remnants of the slave system still exercised a certain function in China's society and economy, etc., etc.

IV

In the problem of the periodization of the history of the ancient period of China there is still another question, which is that of the buds of the elements of capitalism in China. This question is also concerned with the time at which Chinese feudal society first began to break up. Among Chinese historians of the past, very few have made specialized studies of it until most recently, when the period background of the *Dream of the Red Chamber* was debated and gave rise to broadened debate.

Whether China had buds of capitalism — this has not constituted the question. What has constituted the question is at what time these budding elements of capitalism first emerged. On this point there are also different views.

One opinion maintains that the first budding of elements of capitalism can be dimly seen in distant Southern Sung (1127–1279) and early Yüan (late 13th century). But proponents of this then add that the workers of that time seem not yet to have undone the ties of the feudal guilds, and whether the relations of production in the handicraft quarters were capitalistic relations or not it is still very difficult to say.

Another opinion maintains that buds of

capitalist elements first emerged in early Ming (later half of the 14th century). Proponents of this point out that from the demands of the market in early Ming emerged capitalists who provided tools of production and raw materials, and even workers who hired out their labor. Therefore that time, aside from the feudal exploitation by landlords of peasants, also produced the exploitative relations of capitalists against workers.

Another opinion maintains that buds of capitalism first emerged in the *Cheng-te* and *Chia-ching* periods of Ming (from early to middle 16th century). Proponents of this assert that the fields of a large part of the agriculture of that time changed to the production of fibres and other raw materials, that private land ownership developed rapidly, that manager-landlords appeared, and that the public duty system began to change and come apart. Along a strip of the Chiang-nan coast appeared contractual relations between primary producers and landowners. In handicrafts, owing to the development of domestic and foreign markets, the weaving industry and ceramic industry developed at a flying pace. At the end of the 16th century, Soochow had at least some 10,000 workers. But proponents of this point out also that hired workers of the time still were bound by an obligatory work system.

Another opinion maintains that the buds of elements of capitalism correspond to the period from *Chia-ching* to *Wan-li* of Ming (the middle of the 16th century to the beginning of the 17th). They assert that this period is the stage of the most notable shift.

Another opinion maintains that the conditions of society and economy before *Wan-li* of Ming, reflected in the area of social customs, basically had no great changes, and that from *Wan-li* (20th year of the 17th century) on, they changed, because urban industry and commerce developed.

These approaches to views on the question of the buds of the elements of capitalism of China are also unusually diverse.

From the views listed above we can see that the earliest falls in Southern Sung and early Yüan, the latest in *Wan-li* of Ming. The interval of difference is about 500 years.

Just as with the question of transition from slave system to feudal system, China's historians, though their opinions on the buds of the elements of capitalism diverge, hold points in common; that is, all assert that before the invasion of capitalism of foreign countries China already had spontaneous buds of the elements of capitalism. The time, in the general tendency, is asserted to be in the middle period of the Ming dynasty or later.

Owing to the insufficiency of study of the course of development of Chinese society and economy in the Ming and Ch'ing periods, research on the question of the buds of the elements of capitalism is correspondingly still very inadequate. The resolution of this question clearly awaits still deeper study of the history of this period, and especially the study of urban economic functions of the period, handicrafts, agriculture, domestic trade, foreign trade, and other questions.

v

Now to speak of the history of the modern period of China (from the Opium War to the May 4th Movement). The study of the history of the modern period of China is the principal domain of study of Chinese historians. But again, like the history of the ancient period of China, Chinese historians of the past, by the methods they have chosen, have all described in sequence certain striking main events in the modern history of China and have not marked out stages based on the nature of these events. Therefore they have been unable to reflect the essential things in the development of the history of the modern period and have been unable to explain a number of questions.

After the liberation, China's historians also raised the question of the periodization of the history of the modern period. As in the periodization of the history of the ancient period of China, there are also various different views of the periodization of the history of the modern period of China. One view asserts that the history of the modern period of China is the history of the completed class struggle. Therefore, it maintains, the criteria of periods should be basically the signs of class struggle. Accordingly, it takes the three revolutions of China's modern history — the revolution of the Taiping Heavenly Kingdom, the Boxer Movement, and the 1911 Revolution — to be the standards of periodization and divides China's modern history into seven stages. Those who maintain this have criticized in their essays the theory of using the conditions of aggression of foreign force or simply using changes in socio-economic life as standards for periods.

Another opinion asserts that the signs of class struggle are a basically suitable standard of periodization in one socio-economic condition, but when applying this principle to the actuality of China's modern history it is necessary to bear in mind that China's modern society is a half-feudal and half-colonial society. Because of this, it is necessary to pay attention to certain changes in the nature of this society and impossible to take only the high tides of revolution as standards of periods. Those who maintain this agree on not using changes in conditions of aggression of foreign force as standards of periodization, but they assert that aggression and opposition to aggression are two aspects of one event. When establishing periods for half-colonial China, it is not proper to deny the major significance for the periods of Chinese modern history of changes in the nature of aggression. Therefore they assert that the major standards for periods ought to be based on changes in contradictions of the two aspects, external and internal. They divide China's modern history into four periods, using this standard.

Another opinion asserts that standards for the periods of modern Chinese history ought to arise from a combining of socio-economic phenomena and class struggle phenomena. Those who maintain this assert that the "completed class struggle" is not a unique distinguishing feature of the history of the modern period of China but is a feature common to all class societies. They also disagree with substituting a description of the state of the class struggle and changes in class relationships for a concrete analysis of changes in the feudal economic structure. They have also criticized using the development and changes of externally-derived elements in place of an analysis of internal historical laws. Therefore, they divide the history of the modern period of China into five periods, based on their assertions.

Still another opinion asserts that in modern Chinese history, aside from the contradiction between feudalism and the masses of people, there is also a contradiction between the foreign states' power and the Chinese people. Moreover, in a certain sense, these two contradictions also combine into one basic contradiction. That is, the reactionary force in which the foreign powers are the principal form and China's feudal power the secondary makes one aspect of the contradiction, and the masses of the people form another aspect of the contradiction in opposition. Those who maintain this divide Chinese modern history into four periods, based on this way of looking at things.

Thus diverse opinions are seen to exist on the question of the divisions of the history of the modern period of China. To resolve this question also requires research a step further, principally research into the following questions: the formation of the relations of capitalism in China; the accumulation of original capital, its special features and effects on China's economy; new social classes — the formation of the bourgeoisie and proletariat and their part in economic and social life; the development of the political struggle of the peasants, the city poor and the bourgeoisie against Manchu Ch'ing political power, against feudal oppression, and against the slave-domination of foreign capital over the Chinese people; the concrete forms of economic aggression and political aggression of foreign power and, related to this, the course of formation of the compradore bourgeoisie and China's warlord government, etc., etc. Until now the deserved study has still not developed on these questions. The broadened study of China's modern history being developed at present by China's historians will urgently delve deeply to reach solutions of these questions.

VI

Finally to speak of study of the contemporary history of China. That China's historians undertake the study of the contemporary history of China with truly great gusto is easily explained. It is because precisely this contemporary period, owing to the strong development of the Chinese people's revolutionary movement, has brought special strength to the international effects of historical events generated in China in this period. Therefore, to study questions of Chinese contemporary history has the most realistic scientific and political significance.

The area of study of Chinese contemporary history may be said to have just been opened. Hu Ch'iao-mu's [prominent Communist publicist, b. 1905] *Thirty Years of the Communist Party of China* has opened a straight road for the study of this area. Other than this, there are also some works of Chinese historians who have given historical-materialist explanations of some key questions in China's modern history.

In the area of study of Chinese contemporary history the question of periods has also been raised. Hu Ch'iao-mu in his work, on the basis of the writings of Mao Tse-tung and some major documents of the Central Committee of the Chinese Communist Party, makes four periods in Chinese contemporary history, according to the revolutionary war. Moreover, he has explained some questions in their essentials embodying fundamental principles in contemporary history.

In regard to the periods of Chinese contemporary history, there have not yet been any divergent opinions. But this is not to say that in certain concrete problems there have not been or cannot again be questions requiring study and debate. For example, mutual contradictions in China between the international environment and foreign powers in the last thirty years. Again, changes in domestic economic conditions in the last thirty years, and even changes that have arisen in the position and opposition of the respective classes because of that; the history of the Chinese workingmen's movement and the workers' class struggle, etc., etc. — these questions are objects for study by Chinese historians.

Above are the principal contents of historical study of China in the six years since liberation. Of course aside from this, China's historians have also studied some other historical questions, such as the question of the formation of the Han nation, certain questions in the history of China's minority groups, the question of peasant wars, the question of the evaluation of historical figures, and even some comparatively important questions in the history of Chinese thought; and they have achieved certain results in the study of these fields.

It must be pointed out that the achievement of these results is inseparable from the leadership of the Chinese Communist Party and the writings of Chairman Mao Tse-tung. Chairman Mao Tse-tung's writings have not only made precise and detailed historical-materialist analyses of several fundamental questions of the history of the Chinese modern period, they have also given extremely crucial explanations of certain key questions in the history of the Chinese ancient period. Therefore his writings have established in respect to China a solid theoretical foundation for Marxist historiography.

VII

Dear friends, since the liberation China's historical study has seen some work, but this work, even in terms of the needs of the people of New China, is still inadequate. The rank of our historical science is still very junior; the level of our scholarship and theory still very low. We have many tasks that must be done and still are not done, many that are still not done well. In order to advance the tasks of our historical studies to a further stage, our studies must look to the studies of advanced scientists abroad.

China's historians fervently love their own cultural heritage and the fruits of their own labor. At the same time they also have extraordinary respect for the achievements of foreign historians. Therefore, in the six years since the founding of the People's Republic of China, we have advanced scholarly intercourse and cooperation in the area of historical studies as well as other scientific studies with very many states. With historians of the Soviet Union as well as the people's democratic states we have achieved increasingly close ties and cooperation. It has reached the point that over two months ago from today at the Western European Sinologists' conference held at Leyden, Holland, we also established contact with historians of Western Europe, the Americas, and Australia, including historians of the United States, and formed ties, preparing to advance co-operation a further step. These international contacts, ties, and cooperation are truly of no small benefit, as far as we are concerned.

Japan's historians and China's historians have maintained close ties from the ancient past. Moreover, they have also a very long history and have achieved very good results in the study of Chinese history. This is very generally known among China's historians. Only in the most recent very brief period were the ties between us broken. This, in terms of both parties, could not but be a loss. Now we have had the opportunity of visiting Japan and also of meeting Japan's historians. This is a very good beginning for cooperation between us hereafter in tasks of historical study. China's historians welcome this beginning with great passion and fervently hope that the friendliness and academic intercourse between us will, from this starting point, advance to further strength and development.

Dear friends, allow me, representing China's historians, to express again our friendliness toward Japan's historians. Let us join together in the face of truth and dedicate our labors to the development of Sino-Japanese historical science and the exalted task of world peace.

V. ORIENTAL DESPOTISM

Imperial China—
A "Complex" Hydraulic (Oriental) Society

KARL A. WITTFOGEL

In contrast to the unilinear, universal, and necessarily progressive development posed by some modern theorists of Chinese history stands the theory of a special Asiatic or Oriental society, the existence of which implies that more than one course of development, as well as stagnation or regression, is possible for societies. Since the seventeenth century, exponents of this view have included China in their analyses of "Eastern" society in general. Their interpretation, owing to the emphasis placed on the changelessness of the societies, raised little need of periodization. It also paid little attention to intermediate changes which, though less than epoch-making, may have occurred within the overall framework of the Asiatic order.

Karl A. Wittfogel has replaced the simple theory of Oriental ("hydraulic") society, by one using a more differentiated concept of institutional development in the Oriental world in general and in China in particular. According to him, Oriental societies may move from a "primitive" (tribal) to a "simple" state-centered hydraulic society (determined by the rise of an "agromanagerial" state) and thereafter to "semi-complex" and "complex" orders, characterized by an increasing differentiation of private property and property-based classes. According to Dr. Wittfogel this development went particularly far early in China, where a "complex" Oriental society prevailed roughly from the third century B.C., with temporary regressions into a "semi-complex" order and with conspicuous changes between indigenous (purely Chinese) and conquest dynasties.

Professor Wittfogel (b. 1896) has been Director of the Chinese History Project since 1939 — first at Columbia University and then at the University of Washington. He has been Professor of Chinese History in the University of Washington since 1947 and Visiting Professor of Chinese History at Columbia University in 1964.

TRADITIONAL China was an agrarian society which experienced a significant development of handicraft and commerce. In this respect, China was similar to medieval Europe and to certain pre-Hellenistic civilizations of the northern and western Mediterranean. However, while these Western agrarian civilizations ultimately lost their societal identity, Chinese society perpetuated its basic features for millennia. And while medieval Europe saw a commercial and industrial revolution that led to the rise of an industrial society, traditional China never underwent such changes.

Obviously, when characterizing societal structures, it is not enough to speak of agri-

Karl A. Wittfogel, "Chinese Society: An Historical Survey," in The Journal of Asian Studies, Vol. XVI, No. 3 (May, 1957), pp. 343–364. The author has made a number of refinements of the original article, and they are included here with his permission. Copyright by the author.

culture, handicraft, and trade in general. We must consider their ecological and institutional setting and the specific human relations involved in their operation.

Chinese society originated in the middle and lower Yellow River basin under semi-arid conditions. In this agricultural setting agricultural man created a stable economy by manipulating water productively and protectively (for the purposes of irrigation and flood control); and whenever these tasks transcended the strength of individuals or local groups, he did so by means of large work teams directed by the government. I suggest that farming based on such large-scale waterworks be designated *"hydraulic* farming," and that it be differentiated from *"hydro-*agriculture" (small-scale irrigation farming), and, of course, from rainfall farming. I also suggest that a government managing such an agriculture be designated a "hydraulic government," and a society dominated by it a "hydraulic society."

Thus hydraulic society is a special type of agrarian society. Its peculiarities rest on a number of major conditions:

(1) *Cultural:* the knowledge of agriculture.

(2) *Environmental:* aridity or semi-aridity and accessible sources of water supply, primarily rivers, which may be utilized to grow rewarding crops, especially cereals, in a water-deficient landscape. A humid area in which edible aquatic plants, especially rice, can be grown is a variant of this environmental pattern.

(3) *Organizational:* large-scale cooperation.

(4) *Economic:* large-scale (water) feeding activities and irrigation agriculture.

(5) *Protective:* the productive hydraulic activities are usually supplemented by works of flood control that in certain countries, such as China, may be more comprehensive than the irrigation works proper.

(6) *Political:* the organizational apparatus of the hydraulic order is either initiated, or quickly taken over, by the leaders of the commonwealth who direct its vital external and internal activities — military defense and maintenance of peace and order.

(7) *Social:* stratification separating the men of the hydraulic government from the mass of the "people." The rise of a professional, full-time bureaucracy distinguishes *primitive* hydraulic society (headed mostly by part-time functionaries) from the state-centered forms of hydraulic societies (headed by full-time officials), which may have no important secondary classes based on mobile and immobile private property (*simple* hydraulic society), or which may have secondary classes based on mobile private property, such as craftsmen or merchants (*semi-complex* hydraulic society), or secondary classes based on both mobile and immobile private property (*complex* hydraulic society).

The hydraulic type of an agrarian society was not confined to China. Historical evidence indicates that agrarian civilizations with government-directed water control originated several thousand years before the Christian era in the Near East, in Egypt, and in Mesopotamia. Similarly structured societies emerged early in India, Persia, Central Asia (Turkestan), many parts of Southeast Asia, and in Java, Bali, and ancient Hawaii.

In the Western hemisphere such societies flourished prior to the Spanish conquest in the Andean zone (culminating there in the great irrigation empire of the Incas), in Meso-America (particularly in the region of the Lake of Mexico), and in the southwestern United States in Arizona (Hohokam) and, on a tribal scale, in New Mexico among the Pueblo Indians.

European scholars first recognized the peculiarity of the hydraulic state in the great civilizations of the East. Perpetuating classical Greek ideas about the rule of Asiatic "despots," they came to call it "Oriental despotism." The classical economists who continued to use this term spoke of "Asiatic" or "Oriental" societies.

Since the hydraulic civilizations which are spatially most extended and historically most consequential actually originated east of the continent whose scholars conceptualized this phenomenon, the designation "Oriental society" seems legitimate in that it reflects an important geo-historical fact. However, it does not suggest a specific type of human action as do the terms "feudal" and "industrial" society. For this reason I employ the term "hydraulic society" preferably, if interchangeably, with "Oriental society."

I. EARLY CHINA — A SIMPLE AGROMANAGERIAL ("HYDRAULIC") SOCIETY

Contemplating the rise of Chinese civilization in the light of our knowledge of the varieties of agrarian society, I find V. Gordon Childe's concept of an "urban" revolution misleading, and this for the following reasons. Among non-hydraulic agrarian peoples, such as the Germanic tribes, a social stratification separating the nobles and commoners preceded the rise of towns by many centuries. In the same way the emergence of a hydraulic ruling class frequently involved, not the creation of towns, but only of palaces and/or ceremonial centers. This obviously was the case in Hawaii, and also in certain hydraulic regions of ancient America.

Chinese proto-historical legends, more specific than those of ancient Egypt and Mesopotamia, tell of several hydraulic culture heroes — Yao, Shun, and Yü — who tried to control the waters in the Yellow River basin. These stories fit perfectly the geological conditions of North China. The low-lying plains are cut by rivers that regularly deposit silt, thus gradually raising the river beds, causing periodic inundations and eventually changes in the watercourse. These stories also fit perfectly the region's meteorological conditions. The divination texts of Shang suggest a climate that, although slightly warmer and wetter, presented a seasonal pattern of semi-aridity similar to that existing today. Manifestly whoever wanted to farm effectively in these regions had to irrigate his crops, and who-

ever wanted to live there safely had to harness the ever-threatening rivers.[1]

A few decades ago, serious critics doubted the value of the hydraulic legends for a reconstruction of China's early history because many of them survived only in texts of a relatively late origin. But the Shang divination inscriptions have confirmed the validity of such sources as the *Shih chi* and the *Bamboo Annals* for the Shang period.[2] Since the climate at that time was semi-arid, as it is today, and since the Shang state was located in the North Chinese lowlands where the erection of large dikes is necessary for permanent living, the Shang rulers must have engaged in extensive hydraulic activities.

All these considerations make it likely that even the pre-Shang data contain elements of historical truth. The Great Yü, who in the proto-historical records is credited with taming the waters of the Yellow River lowlands and who is associated with the proto-historical Hsia dynasty (allegedly situated in Shansi), may well have been a local culture hero whose accomplishments were later depicted as having benefited all-under-heaven. In the twenties, Ku Chieh-

---

[1] Richthofen complicated his analysis of the hydraulic conquest of the Great North Chinese Plain by relying on a relatively late source, the *Yü kung*. But his statement that the alluvial lowlands of the Northern Plain could be settled only after the completion of comprehensive dike works [see Ferdinand Freiherr von Richthofen, *China, Ergebnisse eigener Reisen und darauf gegründeter Studien* (Berlin, 1877), Vol. I, pp. 354ff.] expresses an elementary geo-agricultural truth which is valid independently of the date of origin of the *Yü kung* [cf. Karl August Wittfogel, *Wirtschaft und Gesellschaft Chinas, Erster Teil, Produktivkräfte, Produktions- und Zirkulationsprozess* (Leipzig, 1931), pp. 281ff.].
[2] The pioneer decipherer of the Shang inscriptions, Wang Kuo-wei, found in these inscriptions most of the names of the Shang rulers given in the *Shih chi* and the *Bamboo Annals*. Where differences appeared, he found the "suspect" *Bamboo Annals* more accurate than the *Shih chi* [Wang Kuo-wei, *Kuan-t'ang chi-lin*, 9.15a]. Such facts, taken in conjunction with the manifestly high development of Shang culture and parallel situations in the prehistory of the Near East, suggest that the references to pre-Shang hydraulic activities in the *Bamboo Annals* and the *Shih chi* may also reflect, despite exaggerations, actual historical events.

kang considered Yü a mythological figure mentioned first in the mid-Chou period. In the thirties he placed him much earlier; and later still he viewed Yü as the divine ancestor of the Hsi Jung, a tribe that is said to have participated in the creation of China's early civilization. One of Professor Ku Chieh-kang's coeditors, Feng Chia-sheng, suggested that Yü may really have constructed substantial hydraulic works in the lower valley of the Fen River in Shansi.

There is no reason to doubt the existence of pre-Shang centers of higher agrarian civilization in North China, and there is no reason to doubt that in this, as in comparable areas, the formative process was not an urban, but a hydraulic revolution.

II. "SEMI-COMPLEX" HYDRAULIC SOCIETY — EXPANSION OF PRIVATE TRADE AND HANDICRAFT

A hydraulic revolution — initiating the rise of a hydraulic society

Such a development is strongly indicated by considerations of geography and climate; it is confirmed by recent discoveries in archaeology and epigraphy. In addition the comparative study of societal conformations reveals significant parallels between the institutions of the first well-described period of Chinese history, Chou, and conditions in other hydraulic societies.

These parallels are suggestive for the highest echelon of the societal pyramid, represented by the relations between the Chou king (Son of Heaven) and the rulers of the various territorial states (the *chu-hou*); they are conclusive for the next highest echelon, represented by the relations between the *chu-hou* and a hierarchy of persons (*ch'ing, ta-fu,* and *shih*) who were assigned land by the territorial ruler they served. The two sets of relations were not contractual as was the case in feudal societies. The superior authority was strong enough to insist on an unconditional subordination, which in the realm of the incipient Chou empire was symbolically recognized, although only imperfectly acted out, while, within the borders of the territorial states, it was theoretically recognized and fully acted out.

The *chu-hou*,[3] who spent most of their time administering their territories, rendered the Chou sovereign the services he requested (essentially military services) unconditionally and without the limitations characteristic of feudal duties: the services of the feudal vassals and lords were generally restricted in time — often to forty days — and in space, participation in the sovereign's campaigns abroad requiring special contractual arrangements. And the payments which the territorial rulers rendered the Son of Heaven, being annual and substantial (essentially precious objects), were much more like taxes than the financial "aids" which the vassals of most countries of feudal Europe rendered their sovereign — when his eldest son was knighted, when his eldest daughter was married, when he went on a crusade, and when he had to be ransomed. The opportunity for the first two aids arose only once during a reign; and for the last two only irregularly and rarely. The services rendered by the *ch'ing, ta-fu,* and *shih* were full-time services rendered not by semi-autonomous lords and knights but by officials. And the land that they held was not a contractually assigned fief but office land given them as a salary. This type of assigned land is documented for many hydraulic societies.

Otto Franke, commenting on the investiture of a territorial ruler by the Son of Heaven, concluded that the Chou ceremony was "a political command or the sovereign's act of grace, not a contract of loyalty and service as in the Frankish Empire." He insisted that a contractual relation between a sovereign and his vassals expressed "a European way of thinking, but it contradicts the spirit of the Chinese concept of the state." Discussing the conditions of territorial power, Henri Maspero found that the territorial rulers of Chou

---

[3] This and the other Chinese terms below designated ranks of nobility in the Chou system. [Editor's note]

kept their serving men in a state of unconditional subordination, and that the land assigned them was a "non-feudal domain," given "to an official as a salary."

However, despite these observations, Franke, Maspero, and others who made similar observations continued to apply a feudal nomenclature to the institutions of Chou China. This is entirely understandable, since several features of simple and semi-complex hydraulic societies actually, or apparently, occur also in feudal society, and since the only method of assigning service land familiar to Western scholars was that of enfeoffment.

The contrast between this attitude and that taken by the Communist ideologists is manifest. The Communist claim that Chou China was a slave-holding society is part of a politically motivated effort to present history as a unilinear, irresistible developmental process; and those who established this developmental scheme, Lenin prominent among them, definitely knew better. Different from them, independent scholars who viewed Chou China as feudal proceeded in good faith. They were employing general scientific principles which would enable them (or their successors) freely to re-examine the issue of Chou society, if changed circumstances so recommended. And this is the situation today. Our growing knowledge of Oriental institutions demands a new approach to the decisive social relations of Chou China. It establishes these relations as elements, not of a feudal, but of an Orientally despotic order. And it compels us to perceive the constructional, organizational, and acquisitive peculiarities of imperial China as consistently arising from those of Chou society.[4]

[4] In my earlier writings I also called Chou a feudal society, although I soon pointed to significant hydraulic trends in Chou and pre-Chou China [Wittfogel 1931, pp. 281ff.]. The systematic study of hydraulic societies induced me to abandon my original view, not because it showed that the transition from a non-hydraulic to a hydraulic society was unlikely — on the contrary, it provided new evidence for such a crossing of the institutional divide [Karl A. Wittfogel,

III. "COMPLEX" HYDRAULIC SOCIETY — PRIVATE PROPERTY SPREADS TO THE COUNTRYSIDE

Institutional Roots and Patterns

The constructional, organizational, and acquisitive operations of hydraulic society are fairly well documented for the periods of the Spring and Autumn Annals and the Warring States. During this time the despotic claims of the Chou dynasty lost their reality, except within the Chou domain itself, while the orientally despotic order assumed a more flexible, and more effective, shape in the territorial states, especially in the country of Ch'in, which ultimately unified China.

Oriental Despotism (New Haven, 1957), pp. 207ff.] — but because the Chinese system of land tenure and social structure fitted the hydraulic pattern of service land and non-contractual subordination rather than the contractual and conditional pattern of feudal relations.

In his recent thoughtful account of early China, Professor E. Reischauer hesitates to call Chou feudal: "The early Chou system was at most only proto-feudal, and the feudal elements decreased rather than grew in the later centuries of the Chou era" [Edwin O. Reischauer and John K. Fairbank, *East Asia: The Great Tradition* (Boston, 1958), p. 52]. "By the eighth century B.C. the various independent states and the organization within these states showed only occasional semi-feudal elements." And while he assumes rainfall agriculture for the Shang period (without, it would seem, taking into account the climatological evidence that indicates the need for flood control in the Shang lowlands), he views the "water control or 'hydraulic' theory" as fitting "neatly with the myths about the culture hero Yü, original controller of the flood waters of China. The use of conscripted labor gangs for great public works, moreover, seems to date far back into Chinese history. . . ."

For an uncritical reproduction of the conventional theory of Chou feudalism, see Derk Bodde, "Feudalism in China," in Rushton Coulborn, ed., *Feudalism in History* (Princeton, 1956), pp. 49ff. In the matter of imperial China, Dr. Bodde does not himself subscribe to the feudal interpretation, but he still finds "merit" in it, since "it centers attention upon vital economic factors such as the political approach may tend to overlook." Unfortunately he does not tell us that private property is at the heart of the feudal interpretation. Nor does he tell us that this interpretation blurs the importance of the bureaucracy as a ruling class in China or that it is a key element in the socio-historical myth so persistently propounded by the Russian and Chinese Communists.

Constructional operations: In China, as in India, large-scale government-managed hydraulic activities combined with many small and medium-sized enterprises to produce a "loose" subtype of the hydraulic system. Having previously given a comprehensive survey of this system, I need only note here that the Chinese hydraulic economy includes large territorial and interterritorial waterworks. The pattern (Loose I) differs from the less impressive variant of a loose hydraulic pattern (Loose II), of which ancient Mexico is an outstanding example.

In addition to productive and protective hydraulic installations, China built enormous communicational hydraulic works, among them the world's longest artificial waterway, the Grand Canal. Some of the large non-hydraulic constructions, such as city walls, palaces, and temples, are documented since the early Chou days. Others, such as state highways and "long walls," appeared spectacularly at the close of the Chou period.

Organizational operations: The large-scale constructions of hydraulic society led to the development of organizational methods which, properly modified, could be applied also to military affairs and communications.

Since the start of the Chou dynasty, standard armies were orderly bodies with a center and two wings; and discussions of the art of war — as alien to feudalism as they are typical of advanced hydraulic societies — became a general feature in Chou China at least from the sixth century B.C. on. Significantly, the Japanese, who readily repeated what certain Chou authors, such as Sun Tzu, had said on this subject, seriously discussed the art of war only after their feudal period came to an end, that is, under Tokugawa absolutism.[5] In Europe, writings on the art of war appeared first in the Greek city states that had integrated citizen armies, and then again, much later, after the close of the feudal period.

At the end of the Chou period, state highways and the state post were fully developed. In Europe, it was only under postfeudal conditions that a system of highways, a state post, navigation canals, and census-taking became significant.[6]

Acquisitive operations: All hydraulic bureaucracies commandeered a substantial part of the labor and/or the products of labor of their subjects. The most numerous group, the peasants, either rendered corvée labor on "public" land or paid taxes. In Chou China the public fields, as an integral element of a system of regulated village land, was a widespread, although probably not a universal institution. In the fourth century B.C. this system of land tenure was abolished in the territorial state of Ch'in. We do not know whether any, or all, of the other territorial states acted similarly before they were conquered, since the final victor, Ch'in, destroyed their records. But we do know that, in the unified empire, land was bought and sold freely. Among the secondary institutional developments of China the establishment of private landownership at the end of the Chou dynasty is perhaps the most important one. Unfortunately, it is among the least clearly documented.

The rise of independent artisans and merchants seems to have preceded the spread of private landownership by several centuries. The literary records suggest that up to the period of the Spring and Autumn Annals the majority of the professional traders were attached to the various courts and administrative centers.

Thus after a primitive (tribal) hydraulic

---

[5] Delmer M. Brown, "The Impact of Firearms on Japanese Warfare, 1543–98," *FEQ*, No. VII (1948), 236ff. According to a communication from Dr. Marius Jansen (Princeton University) on this topic, "the first integrated treatment of the subject [the art of war] comes in a work by Takeda Shingen [1521–73]."

[6] In Japan an incipient — and frustrated — early hydraulic development produced elements of an orientally despotic system of communications and census-taking. But the rising feudal order prevented the growth of these elements. Like the art of war, they gained in vigor only after the close of the feudal period. See Wittfogel 1957, pp. 198ff.

beginning China moved very slowly from a "simple" hydraulic society (with a regulated land system and little private handicraft and commerce) to a "semi-complex" hydraulic society (which still had a regulated land system, but increased private handicraft and trade) and then quickly to a "complex" hydraulic society with a considerable development of both mobile and immobile private property. Except for a temporary regression to a regulated land system, which lasted from the fifth to the eighth century A.D., China perpetuated itself as a complex hydraulic society throughout the imperial period, that is, roughly speaking, for almost two thousand years. . . .

Conquest Dynasties and Conquest Societies

. . . During the era of the imperial dynasties, conquest played a substantial role in shaping China's societal order. To be sure, Inner Asian tribes had invaded the "Middle Country," *chung-kuo*, in Chou and pre-Chou times. But the "barbarian" pastoralists became a serious threat only when horseback riding increased their mobility (the technique had spread to the Far East by 500 B.C.). They became a truly formidable threat when the stirrup increased their firing and hitting power. During a period of transition, increasingly powerful "barbarians" moved into Chinese territory — in part invited, in part just pushing ahead — to infiltrate, and then overpower their Chinese neighbors. The empire of the Northern [Toba] Wei (386–534) is a particularly instructive example of such an "infiltration dynasty."

The Sui emperors again unified the empire, which had been split into a Chinese South and a barbarian North under the Southern and Northern dynasties. A reorganized and revitalized bureaucracy consolidated China, until a cyclical internal crisis caused the collapse of the T'ang dynasty. On its ruins, the Ch'i-tan tribesmen established on the northeastern periphery of China the first major conquest dynasty, Liao.

The Sung dynasty defended the greater part of China against the Liao armies. But it was less successful against the Jurchen, the tribal successors of the Ch'i-tan, who set up in North China a second conquest dynasty, Chin. Interestingly, they stopped at the edge of the rice area, which eight hundred years previously the Toba horsemen had also found hard to cross.

Even the much stronger Mongols were at the start unable to carry their conquest of China beyond the rice line. But when Kublai Khan overran Southern Sung, the northern "barbarian" conquerors for the first time seized the whole country.

After the collapse of the Ming dynasty this extraordinary feat was repeated by the Manchus, the most sinicized of the barbarian invaders. Different from the essentially pastoral Ch'i-tan and Mongols, but like the Jurchen, the Manchus in their pre-dynastic days engaged in agriculture as well as animal husbandry. In fact, they practiced irrigation farming before they crossed the Great Wall to conquer China.

There would be no need in a sketch of Chinese society to take more than fleeting notice of these waves of conquest if the Chinese had always absorbed their conquerors. That they did so has been claimed by many scholars who found that soon after the establishment of their power the barbarian rulers began to adopt Chinese culture. Conquest, however, is a military and political phenomenon, and to test the validity of the absorption theory we must first determine whether or not the tribal conquerors of China lost their military and political identity after they became the masters of a part or the whole of China.

Examination of the pertinent facts reveals that this failed to happen either in the four major conquest societies of Liao, Chin, Yüan, and Ch'ing, or in such earlier infiltration dynasties as the Toba Wei. In the case of the four later dynasties we can say that in all of them the conquerors maintained a special military machine composed mainly of reliable tribesmen: under the Liao dynasty the *ordu* ("horde"); under the Chin dynasty the *meng-an mo-k'o;* under the Yüan dynasty the Mongol troops; and under the Ch'ing dynasty the "banners."

The tribal conquerors also reserved for themselves the political key positions; and, as a rule, they forbade intermarriage between the conquering group and the Chinese. Thus national distinctions became social distinctions; and the customary Chinese class structure was complicated by new strata, a ruling tribal nobility that ranked above, but worked closely with, the Chinese bureaucracy (which remained indispensable for controlling the Chinese population), and the tribal commoners who, a barbarian nation in arms, stood apart from and above the Chinese commoners.

Summing up, the conquerors, who in varying degrees adopted Chinese culture and folkways, never gave up their superior socio-political position nor, for that matter, their religion. Even the Manchu rulers who faithfully performed the sacred ceremonies of the Chinese state religion continued within the walls of their residences to worship their tribal gods. . . .

Basing ourselves on the fact that the dynasties of conquest (and infiltration) differed socio-politically from the typically Chinese dynasties, we can distinguish the following subdivisions in the history of imperial China (221 B.C.–1912 A.D.):

The Class Structure of China's Complex Hydraulic Society

The typically Chinese dynasties represent a complex pattern of hydraulic society. As stated above, a complex hydraulic society gives considerable leeway to the representatives of private mobile and immobile property. From the days of the Han dynasty on, merchants figured conspicuously in the economy of imperial China; and except for an interlude of about three centuries private landholdings were widespread. But despite the enhancement of the status of rich merchants in the Early Han period (which was short-lived) and despite many peasant revolts (which never threatened the basic despotic order), the forces of private property and enterprise had little influence on the ruling institutions: the hydraulic state, the autocratic power of the sovereign, and the hierarchy of ranking officials and bureaucratic underlings.

It is obvious that the Western concepts of class which have explained supreme social position essentially in terms of private property (of slaves, land, and capital) do not explain the basic stratification of hydraulic society. Under the conditions of hydraulic society, which seems to have shaped the lives of two thirds of mankind, control over the state apparatus rather than the manipulation of private property created supreme power, prestige, and wealth. This

TYPICALLY CHINESE DYNASTIES

1. Ch'in and Han (221 B.C.–220 A.D.)
2. Chinese dynasties during the Period of Disruption (220–581)

4. Sui and T'ang (581–907)
5. Sung (960–1279)

9. Ming (1368–1644)

DYNASTIES OF CONQUEST
(AND "INFILTRATION")

3. Wei [T'o-pa] (386–556) and other northern barbarian dynasties directly before and after.

6. Liao [Ch'i-tan] (907–1125)
7. Chin [Jurchen] (1115–1234)
8. Yüan [Mongol] (1206–1368)

10. Ch'ing [Manchu] (1616–1912)

was so not only in the many hydraulic societies in which private landownership was a minor factor, but also in the much less numerous complex hydraulic societies, among which post-Chou China is outstanding.

In accordance with a trend that also characterizes the less developed private landownership of simple and semi-complex hydraulic societies, the landlords of imperial China were primarily officiating and non-officiating members of the ruling class. In other words, landlordism was in the main *bureaucratic landlordism*. Moreover the non-officiating notables in Chinese society, as in all other hydraulic societies, were primarily former officials and relatives of officials. In China this group was supplemented, from the time of the establishment of the examination system, by holders of official degrees. The higher and middle degrees made their possessors eligible for bureaucratic position.

Western writers have called these notables "gentry," not too fortunately since in the context of European feudalism this designation connotes an aristocratic group with strong landed property. Members of the Chinese gentry usually possessed property, and often much of it; but this property was not strong property[7] even when it consisted of land. For the fragmenting laws of inheritance, which are typical of Oriental despotism, required that all property be split among the heirs, in China essentially among the sons. Such a system combined with polygamy — i.e., generally numerous children — fragmented even large landholdings in a few generations.

Nor was the Chinese gentry part of a multicentered feudal society in which the landed gentry was organized in an "estate" (corporation, *Stand*) strong enough to challenge the ruler. Quite the contrary, the Chinese gentry was the non-officiating

part of the ruling bureaucracy of a single-centered society, which tolerated only one organization, the state. It was a *bureaucratic gentry*, whose members, no matter whether they held land or not, were necessarily oriented toward the holding of government office. . . .[8]

IV. DEVELOPMENTAL PROBLEMS UNDERLYING THE DISINTEGRATION OF TRADITIONAL CHINESE SOCIETY

An Insufficiently Studied Phenomenon

All this makes it easy to understand why nowhere within the hydraulic world did the single-centered agrarian order by its inner forces change into a multicentered industrial society. At the same time it makes it hard to understand why modern social science has concerned itself so little with the very obvious — and very fateful — problem as to how and in what direction these traditionally self-perpetuating orders are today being transformed. Reference to an irresistible "Asian revolution" confuses rather than clarifies the issue. The societal character of this alleged revolution is rarely defined; and hints at a unilinear developmental concept, supposedly suggested by Marx, offer a fictitious answer when a realistic posing of the question is of the essence.

Actually the frequently invoked founding fathers of "scientific socialism" did not claim a unilinear sequence for their major societal conformations. And the Asiatic revolution, as Marx saw it, differed fundamentally from the medieval and post-me-

---

[7] For an early attempt to distinguish the "strong" or "absolute" property that developed in the West from the Eastern forms of ownership see Henry Sumner Maine, *Village Communities in the East and West* (New York, 1889), pp. 158ff., 221ff.

[8] See Chang Chung-li, *The Chinese Gentry* (Seattle, 1955) *passim*. Dr. Hsiao, who in his book, *Rural China*, is not concerned with comparative data, reaches similar conclusions on the Chinese gentry. According to him, its members "gained their special status by acquiring an official rank or position, or by passing one or more series of examinations" [Kung-chuan Hsiao, *Rural China* (Seattle, 1960), p. 574]. In 1931, during the only major open discussion of the Asiatic mode of production, held in the USSR, a spokesman for the Communist Party's "feudal" line crudely rejected the bureaucratic interpretation of the Chinese gentry maintained by the author [see Wittfogel 1957, p. 402].

dieval revolutions of the West in that it came about, not through spontaneous internal changes, but through the impact of external forces, essentially forces of the industrial West.

I suggest calling this process a diversive revolution. Mill and Marx realized that the Asiatic revolution was of this type. It is important to acknowledge their insights, but it is equally important to see that neither of them understood the difficulties involved in such a transformation. Mill and Marx erred because they ascribed to the Western impact an institutional effect which it never achieved in any of the major Old World areas of Oriental society and despotism.

An Incipient Diversive Revolution

What occurred in these areas was a diverse development toward a multicentered society, initiated from the outside and taken up by endogenous forces which, though feeble, had potentials of growth. In the 19th and early 20th century such forces in Russia mustered enough strength to prevail temporarily after the democratic revolution of March 1917.

In India, the transformation promoted by the West did not create a multicentered society, but it did create democratic patterns of government and encourage a variety of anti-totalitarian forces. Today these forces are fighting against increasing odds, since prominent Indian statesmen and intellectuals are identifying themselves with important managerial features of Communist statecraft. . . .

In China, the diversive, West-oriented revolution began during the last phase of Ch'ing rule, and it gained considerable strength after 1912. The movement initiated by the "Literary Renaissance" went far beyond literature proper; it was particularly successful in the sphere of ideas and education. Communists and Communist sympathizers soon played a substantial role in this development.

It scarcely needs emphasizing that many features of Nationalist policy, such as the measures against the remnants of slavery and the trend toward improving the status of women, originated before the Kuomintang and the Communists concluded their first United Front. The Chinese national-revolutionary movement, however, very different from the Turkish, became a major political factor only after the Soviet regime consolidated its territorial and political position. By 1923 Moscow was ready to pursue actively a new type of foreign policy which, operating largely through congenial indigenous forces, multiplied the effect of Soviet diplomacy and economic and military aid.

After the collapse of the United Front in 1927, China's West-oriented transformation proceeded on many levels, supported by the Nationalist government, but impeded and partly frustrated by the ideological activities of the Communists, who, after their crushing defeat in 1927, covertly influenced China's cultural life. During and after the Sino-Japanese War, the Communists again appeared as a major political, military, and ideological factor. The incipient Chinese diversive (democratic) revolution was challenged and eventually defeated by a new type of a totalitarian counterrevolution.

This counterrevolution began as a seemingly cathartic, restorative revolution in that it revitalized the semi-managerial despotic order which, during the twenties and thirties, had been increasingly loosened up. However, new methods of social control at once distinguished the Communist regime from the limited methods of domination employed by the traditional Oriental absolutism. And after the collectivization of agriculture, which in 1955 deprived the mass of all peasants of their land, the qualitatively new character of Chinese society became unmistakably clear. The Communist transformation created a total managerial economy which enabled the ruling bureaucracy to exert total control over the mass of the population.

Like all essential changes in the structure of society this development must be judged in accordance with its significance for three major aspects of human life:

(1) Man's relation to nature (progress in technology and natural science)
(2) Man's relation to his fellowmen (social and political progress)
(3) Man's relation to his inner self (progress in the realm of man's basic insights, convictions, and beliefs)

However great the technical progress, any evaluation of the Communist revolution must be made on the basis of its successes (and failures) within the second and third relations. These are the relations that constitute the core of our existence; and it is within them that man's position under Communism is being abysmally worsened. In terms of human values the Communist revolution, both in Russia and China must be classed as a *retrogressive* revolution.

VI. REFLECTIONS AND RESERVATIONS OF HISTORIANS

The Spirit of Periodization

MIYAZAKI ICHISADA

The selection below comes from a review by Professor Miyazaki of *The Periodization of Chinese History*, a book published after the visit of a Chinese academic mission to Japan, where Chien Po-tsan read the paper translated in an earlier selection and, together with other Chinese, conducted talks with Japanese historians. Professor Miyazaki, in addition to expressing reservations about some of the views expressed in the transcript of the talks, takes the opportunity to state the methods and aims he finds valid in periodization.

FRESH in our memory are the historical studies talks held in various places and centering round Messrs. Chien Po-tsan and Yin Ta on the occasion of the reception of the scholarly mission to Japan led by Mr. Kuo Mo-jo, President of the Academy of Sciences of China, at the close of 1955. . . .

Since Part 1 [of the book] carries the conversations centering on Mr. Chien Po-tsan as well as translating Mr. Chien's manuscript, therein we can know what the central questions of periodization are in China at present. What first strikes us as curious, then, is that the question whether the Western Chou period was feudal is taken up extensively. Yet this is a natural attitude in the historical-materialist view. It need hardly be said that in historical materialism the superstructure is regulated by the substructure. The Chinese political form closest to Occidental feudalism is, after all, *feng-chien* [in the 20th century commonly translated "feudalism"]. If it were established that the *feng-chien* system

of the Duke of Chou had been effected in the Western Chou period, underneath must have been the structure that brought it about (if the system of the Duke of Chou were denied, of course, it would be quite a different story). This course is more reasonable, I think, than to establish, like Japanese scholars, a feudal period without feudalism above.

The question of periodization, however, is the most general and at the same time the most relative question. It is necessary to see Chinese history as one part of world history as a whole and also to achieve a balance relative to other regions. Of course in the historical-materialist view, "feudalism" is a general developmental notion, but if in contrast to Europe's entering a feudal period in the 4th century, China's entrance into a feudal period is put from about the 12th century B.C., there is a difference of ten-some centuries between them. In what is the reason to be sought that China was so far ahead in the ancient period? If that be admitted, moreover, the

From *Rekishigaku kenkyū* 12, December 1957, No. 214, pp. 43–45. Translated by the editor. Used by permission of the author.

empire of the preceding ancient period must be sought in sparse Yin. Then, once into the feudal period, if that goes on for at least three thousand years, is it not helpless against statements about the stagnant nature of Chinese society? Indeed, when we see Mr. Chien Po-tsan not acknowledging the culture-diffusion theory and denying even the theory of the western origin of polychrome pottery, we assume that his purpose is to say that in China there were stages of development of an independent Chinese history. We feel extraordinary misgivings about such an attitude. We hail from our heart the success of the anti-colonial movement, but we are disturbed when next an old sinocentric thinking is revived. Mr. Chien has said that before his visit to Japan, Japanese and Chinese scholarly circles were almost without intercourse, but in fact Japan's historical studies have exerted reasonably great influence in China. It is only explicitly that they are not cited. In the current Chinese journals we read, it is often the style to cite in the text only Marx, in the footnotes the primary sources, and to amputate anything else. This is a return of the *Record of Beliefs Investigated*.[1] I hope keenly that my fears may end as groundless. . . .

In Part 2 my views are referred to from time to time, but since regrettably my ideas are not correctly transmitted, I may be permitted a word of explanation here. The basis of my periodization begins from the position that the division into three periods, ancient, medieval, and modern in Marx's formula, is inadequate. This tripartite method took as its standard the later-advancing region, Europe. In regions that have gone through a longer historical era, a Z-section, so to speak, must be inserted and a division made into four periods, such as — any names will do — ancient period, middle age, modern age, and

most modern age. Even in European history, if examined in detail, between the feudal period of the so-called middle ages and the capitalism of the modern period, one more intervening stage exists. This is what I call the modern age, which is clear in the western part and vague in the later-advancing zone of the eastern part. Since the feudal system and capitalism overlapped in the Germany in which Marx was born and the Russia in which a Communist revolution first succeeded, nothing is between them. But in China, which was to some degree earlier advanced than Europe, the existence of this period appears most clearly. Because the European periodization was applied as it was to other regions without this relationship being observed, incoherence arose. It was exactly equivalent to dressing an adult in children's clothing. May not the repeated appearance of idealistic theories in the name of historical materialism come from the incoherence at its root?

I, of course, am not a materialist. Yet in my fashion, I have admired historical materialism. On the whole, as one system, one doctrine, discharges a certain duty, it then becomes an obstacle hindering development. That historical materialism has played an important role I, too, recognize. But the present world is developing at a truly great rate of speed. It is so with the development of scholarship as well. One year of the present corresponds to a number of years, even a number of decades, of the past. Now, when it has been understood that Marx's theory of revolution must also be developed with the times, has the time not come when we must correct also the formula of stages of development of human society? Historical materialism is a thing from the previous century; the study of history is a thing human beings have transmitted for several tens of centuries. I should like to think that the study of history is greater than historical materialism.

Asked to introduce, I have criticized more than I have introduced, and the crit-

[1] *K'ao hsin lu,* by Ts'ui Shu (1740–1816), who aimed to correct the record of ancient history on the assumption that only the Classics and the sages were largely unassailable. [Editor's note]

icism has resulted in a busy statement of an opposite theory; but seeing that I almost never write in this journal, I do not

at all think that my views, individual though they be, will be useless to the readers.

The Beguilement of Historicism

E. G. PULLEYBLANK

E. G. Pulleyblank (b. 1922), originally trained in Classics in Canada, turned to the study of Chinese and has become best known for his work in the history of the T'ang dynasty. He has been Professor of Chinese at the University of Cambridge since 1953. In the selection below he warns that Chinese history may not profitably fit into Western patterns and that a better understanding of world history may come from disciplined use of analogies and the discovery of actual historical connections.

IN spite of all that has been done [in Chinese studies] by those who have gone before, working often with very inadequate resources and amid apathy, it must be confessed that the impact on the public has not really been very great, not as great as in France, say, not anything like as great as it ought to be in view of China's importance. Anyone who devotes himself to the study of Chinese must become inured to the scarcely concealed amusement and the facetious comments with which this information is not infrequently received. China as the land where everything is upside down or back to front, where the men wear pigtails and talk in sing-song, to mention only the more innocuous stereotypes, is part of our folklore and as such seems not worthy of serious attention by adults. I have met this attitude even in enlightened Cambridge circles but I fancy it is becoming less common than it may once have been. Present-day China is a force in the world that demands to be taken very seriously.

And regarding the past also, our Western complacency is no longer quite so sure of itself. We are, I think, becoming gradually conscious that human history — or all that counts of human history — has not flowed in one main stream from Classical Greece and Rome to modern Western Europe. In our contracted twentieth-century world we are forced out of our parochial attitude, to recognize other peoples and cultures from a standpoint of equality which few if any of our immediate ancestors were capable of adopting. Many thinking people today would accept the principle that a proper understanding of our present world and how it came into being must take into account the past of the whole of mankind and not merely of that part of it with which we particularly identify ourselves. There are, it is true, those who strongly advocate a contrary point of view, who maintain, that is, that Western Christian civilization is so uniquely valuable that nothing else counts by comparison. Yet the fact that they have to advocate this point of view consciously and explicitly and cannot merely take it

From E. G. Pulleyblank, *Chinese History and World History* (Cambridge, 1955), pp. 4–36. Reprinted by permission of Cambridge University Press.

for granted shows that the old self-confidence has been shaken.

To say that it has been more than shaken would be, perhaps, to indulge in wishful exaggeration. Old habits of mind die hard, especially when firmly allied to ignorance. To acknowledge, when pressed, the desirability of widening one's historical horizons does not mean that one will proceed to the enormous effort of will that is required to accomplish it. The commonest way in which persons in the West who write books called "histories of the world" dispose of China is virtually to ignore it altogether or at any rate, to treat its history as something entirely external and irrelevant. The standard treatment seems to be to allow China two or three pages appended to "ancient empires" and not to mention the name again until it becomes the object of Western politics in modern times. The author of a recently published book in which this pattern is followed complacently remarks in his preface that although, since his book is directed to Western readers, the main emphasis has been on Europe and America, the East has by no means been neglected. It is rather uncommon nowadays to find no mention at all of China in a work of this sort but one has only to turn to special histories of such subjects as war, banking or political thought to find authors who are content to assume that such things did not exist east of the Mediterranean lands.

The reason for this failure is not merely lack of knowledge, formidable as this is. It is rather the lack of the means of fitting the vast mass of detail of Chinese history into familiar patterns of Western history. For it obviously will not help very much simply to take Chinese history as it has been narrated by its own historians and to add it on in an arithmetical way to one's account of European history. To be rendered intelligible to Western readers Chinese history must undergo a process of translation, and not of words alone but of whole concepts and systems of concepts. Further, if it is to be made congruent with

Western history, our concepts for dealing with Western history must also come under criticism and new concepts must be devised wihch will be adequate to render each culture intelligible in terms of the other.

Faced with a problem of such magnitude it is not surprising that most historians of the academic sort have chosen to ignore it as far as possible. It is to the philosophic historians that one must turn to find any serious attempt to give Chinese history its proper place and to integrate it into a genuine world history. Yet, although those philosophic historians in the West who have turned their attention to China have at least recognized its existence and, to a certain degree, its importance, they have, on the whole, merely been able to apply to Chinese history preconceived notions which make it intelligible only at the expense of distorting it out of recognition; and the Chinese and Japanese who have attempted the same sort of thing have generally adopted as their basic framework systems devised in the West. The result has been that to a very considerable extent the inclusion of Chinese history in such world histories has not had its proper effect in enlarging and enriching them but has simply provided illusory support for previously held dogmas. Without attempting anything like an exhaustive treatment of the subject I should like to discuss briefly some of the principal systems of world history in which Chinese history has found a place in order to illustrate such failings before I suggest what seems to me to be a more fruitful approach.

If we are to see how the problem has developed we must go back to the seventeenth and eighteenth centuries when knowledge about Chinese historical traditions first began to be diffused among learned Europeans. The name that first comes to mind is that of Voltaire. There had been others before him who had tried to reconcile Chinese chronology with that of the Bible or to identify the legendary emperor Fu-hsi with Noah, or to prove that Chinese was the primitive language. Leibniz especially had been interested in all matters pertaining to China and had gone so far as to write that if Chinese chronology were to be accepted one would have to revise the date of the creation. He urged his Jesuit correspondents to translate Chinese historical source materials, since in order to understand man's development it was not sufficient to study the history of Greece and Rome. But it was Voltaire who in his *Essai sur les mœurs,* which has been called the first genuine attempt at a world history, boldly abandoned a Europe-centered viewpoint and began his book with China.

Voltaire, the foremost among the sinophiles in eighteenth-century France, looked upon China as the model of a society governed by reason. Though he admitted certain imperfections such as a backwardness in mathematics and the natural sciences, he was loud in his praise of Confucianism with its rationalistic ethics and its freedom from priestly mystifications. He warmly defended the government of China against the imputation of being despotic put upon it by his contemporary Montesquieu.

Yet much as one admires Voltaire's freedom from European prejudice, one is forced to admit that his picture of China and his arguments based on it have their real meaning only in his own European context. His actual knowledge of China was very limited and one-sided. It was gained almost exclusively from the partisan accounts of the Jesuits, engaged in the famous Rites Controversy and concerned, by demonstrating the conformity of Confucianism with natural religion, to justify as against their opponents of the other missionary orders the expedient compromises with Chinese customs by which they had managed to gain a foothold at the court of Peking. Voltaire was only too glad to turn the Jesuits' weapons against the whole Catholic Church and to take their eulogy of China as evidence of the superiority of natural religion

over the priest-ridden and superstitious religion of Europe.

Voltaire's attitude was typical of the enthusiasm for China that prevailed in his day, but contrary opinions were not lacking, even among liberal thinkers. Montesquieu's views have already been mentioned. He dissented from the view propounded by the Jesuits and Voltaire that Chinese government was the humane and enlightened rule of philosopher mandarins and instead saw it as an example of naked despotism. In so far as he drew on the harsher accounts of sailors and traders to supplement those of the Jesuits, Montesquieu had a more realistic picture of China than did his opponents. Yet it has been shown that his motive in going to these other sources was in order to make China fit into the place he wished to assign it in his world picture. Montesquieu looked upon forms of government as geographically determined — in large states despotism, in medium-sized states, monarchy, and in small states, republicanism. To each of these forms of government corresponded as *principe* — fear, honour or virtue as the case might be. Under the influence of the sinophiles Montesquieu at first looked upon China as a despotism in which the *principe* of fear was modified by honour and virtue, but later he clearly found this too damaging to his system and he drew on hostile accounts to show that fear was the only ruling principle. The idea of China as a society in which the whole population lay in a state of abject slavery subject to the capricious will of the ruler, though advocated in a humane and liberal cause, has had a pernicious effect on later European attitudes which is not wholly eradicated even today.

Before the end of the eighteenth century the inevitable reaction against the excesses of the earlier enthusiasm for China had brought an end to the vogue known as *sinomanie* and the new and closer relations which began to develop between Europe and China from the beginning of the nineteenth century onwards did not at first lead to greater mutual respect. While the Manchu dynasty went into a decline following the glories of K'ang-hsi and Ch'ien-lung, the British, in the full tide of the industrial revolution and full of arrogant self-confidence, demanded and ultimately enforced the opening up of the Celestial Empire to foreign trade. The Protestant missionaries who came with them did not concern themselves with cultivating the governing classes in the hope of converting the nation from above as the Jesuits had done but, like the Dominicans and Franciscans, turned their attentions to the common people, whom they regarded as benighted heathens, roughly on a par with tribal Africans or South Sea cannibals.

In Europe itself, though we must recognize the beginnings of serious academic sinology which were laid in the early decades of the century by Abel Rémusat and Klaproth, greater familiarity did not at first induce a greater appreciation. Even Voltaire had been led to speculate on the difference in the constitutional endowment of the Chinese from that of the Europeans which had made them come to civilization at one bound yet had prevented them from progressing further, and he had sought reasons for this lack of progress in the respect paid to antiquity and the nature of the Chinese written language. To those who came after him belief in the reputed antiquity of all things in China, fostered by an uncritical acceptance of Chinese statements, was held to its discredit and the myth of the pristine excellence of China was replaced by the still familiar myth of the unchanging East, irretrievably sunk in stagnant semi-barbarism, as opposed to a dynastic and triumphant West.

This was the view of China which Hegel found admirably suited to his purpose when he wished to paint his picture of history marching majestically across the map of Eurasia with the sun to culminate in nineteenth-century Prussia. "The first phase —

that with which we have to begin — is the East. . . . It is the childhood of History." "On the one side we see duration, stability — Empires belonging to mere space, as it were — *unhistorical history* [my italics]; as for example, in China. . . . On the other side, the Form of Time stands contrasted with this spatial stability. The states in question, without undergoing any change in themselves, or in the principle of their existence, are constantly changing their position towards each other." And again — "[The] distinguishing feature of the character of the Chinese people is, that everything which belongs to Spirit — unconstrained morality, in practice and in theory, Heart, inward Religion, Science and Art properly so called — is alien to it." And so on — the details of the picture are skilfully sketched in and interpreted in such a way as to fit the general pattern. Even the undeniable skill of Chinese craftsmen is mere superficial cleverness which Europeans, just because of their intelligence, cannot imitate.

This sort of claptrap would be scarcely worthy of our attention were it not for the influence which it has had and continues to have to the present day. Of all Hegelians the most influential has been Karl Marx. Marx, whose attention was focused on Europe and the hope of a socialist revolution there, did not have very much to say about the position of China in the scheme of world history, but from his references to China it seems clear that he had fundamentally the same attitude to it as had Hegel — with the usual turning upside down, that is, the substitution of a dialectic based on economic factors for that of abstract (or should I say concrete) ideas. Thus in journalistic articles Marx speaks of China as "semi-barbarian" "vegetating in the teeth of time" and on another occasion he alludes to the "hereditary stupidity" of the Chinese. About the same time Engels spoke of "China, the rotting semi-civilization of the oldest State in the world." In his theoretical writings Marx postulated five stages of human history corresponding to the Asiatic, ancient, feudal, capitalist and socialist modes of production, and it seems clear that the Asiatic stage is simply his reinterpretation of Hegel's first stage, the Orient. Later, under the influence of the anthropologist Morgan, Marx and Engels spoke rather of the "gens" society as the stage preceding ancient slave society, but since they found examples of this in existing communal villages in India, it is natural to suppose that they equated Asiatic society (or, in its political form, Oriental despotism) with the first form of the state erected on the basis of primitive communism. In the twenties of this century when the practical problem arose of fitting Communist theory to the actual situation in China, this theory gave rise to serious difficulties and I shall consider presently the arguments and conflicting theories that developed. First, however, I wish to discuss briefly certain non-Marxist post-Hegelian treatments of China.

Oswald Spengler's conception of China gave a good deal more value to Chinese history than Hegel had done, for instead of postulating a single organic historico-geographico-evolutionary development of all human history, Spengler looked upon history as a series of separate, finite, organic life-cycles of culture of which Chinese culture was one. China had therefore had a history which was as valid as any other; but as Chinese culture had been dead for nearly two thousand years, the history of all the events and cultural achievements since that time had been, in a Hegelian sense, unhistorical. To a sinologist this is only a less monstrous distortion than Hegel's. Moreover, Spengler's treatment of that part of Chinese history which he acknowledges to be historical amounts to fitting it on to the procrustean framework provided by his conception of the course of Classical and European history.

It may seem ungrateful for an orientalist to carp at Professor Toynbee when he has done so much to attack the Europe-centeredness of European historians. Yet there is more than a whiff of Hegelian brimstone and quite a strong odor of Spengler in his formulations about China. He neatly got out of Spengler's monstrous proposition that Chinese culture has been dead since the Han dynasty by deriving a daughter Far Eastern civilization from the earlier Sinic civilization, through the intermediation of Buddhism as a Universal Church. Far Eastern civilization in its two branches, China and Japan, is conceived of as dying just at the time when the West appears on the scene — so that the period of unhistorical history is reduced to zero, yet one does not have to entertain the unwelcome metaphysical proposition that a living civilization is being destroyed by external agency. But surely *the* great contrast between Chinese and Western history is to be found in the relative continuity and absence of sharp breaks in the former as compared to the latter. Many of Toynbee's analogies are, I admit, very suggestive — as long as they are not taken seriously — but if they are taken seriously they distort Chinese history by forcing on to it conceptions drawn from the Christian world and its antecedents that are quite foreign to it.

Now I should like to say something about some ideas, clearly ultimately Hegelian in origin, that have influenced and still influence the treatment of Chinese history in Japan, and which seem also to have penetrated into certain non-Marxist circles on the mainland during the first quarter or so of this century. Evolution was very much in the air when Japan began to adopt Western ideas in the second half of the nineteenth century and as might have been expected the idea of progress in history was soon enthusiastically taken up by historians there. It may seem curious to an outsider that the form in which it took hold and in which it has persisted with a strange tenacity is that of the threefold division of history into ancient, medieval and modern. To cite an early example, in 1878 we find a Mr. Oka Sennin writing a preface to a book called (*Bankoku Shiki*) "Historical Records of All Countries" by Oka-moto Kansuke, in which he undertakes to explain the significance of the fact that Westerners divide history into ancient, me-dieval and modern. He explains that West-erners see history as a progressive develop-ment in which each stage represents an advance in civilization and he contrasts this favourably with the Chinese and Japanese view which is hostile to progress since it looks back to a golden age in the past from which later periods represent only a de-cline. By the end of the nineteenth cen-tury it had become standard practice in the middle school curricula for all three branches of history, Japanese, Eastern (i.e. Chinese) and Western, to divide into an-cient, medieval and modern, with some-times a period called recent or contempo-rary added at the end. Except in the case of Western history one cannot at first de-tect any evolutionary significance attached to these divisions. They were made arbi-trarily where it seemed most convenient. In the case of Chinese history the usual division was to make ancient history end with the unification by Ch'in in 221 B.C. and to place the end of medieval history either at the beginning of the Sung dy-nasty or at the Mongol conquest. The pe-riod since 1644 under the reigning Manchu dynasty was classed as Recent.

In 1914 the eminent Kyoto sinologist Naitō Torajirō published a book called *Shina-ron* ("Discussion on China") in which he attempted for the first time to give China a periodization which should not be simply an arbitrary division for the sake of convenience but which should have a genuine inner significance. As well as being a considerable scholar in both Japa-nese and Chinese studies, Naitō was a journalist and had served his country as a diplomat in Manchuria and Peking. He had more than a disinterested academic in-terest in formulating his views on Chinese history for he was concerned to decide at what stage China was in her historical de-velopment in order to be able to predict the outcome of the nationalist revolution

and the manoeuvres of Yüan Shih-k'ai to make himself emperor. One need feel no surprise that his conclusions, both then and later in the 1920's, were curiously satis-factory to Japanese nationalist aims. He was merely following in the path of his German predecessor Hegel.

Naitō's main intuition was that China had reached its modern age in the early part of the Sung dynasty in the tenth and eleventh centuries A.D. That is, in Naitō's conception, it had changed from an aristo-cratic society in which the ruler was only the first among his nobles, to a despotism in which the ruler had absolute power and stood far above his subjects, who were, how-ever, more nearly equal and free among themselves. He clearly had in mind an analogy with the change in Europe from feudalism to royal absolutism as, for ex-ample, in France in the sixteenth and sev-enteenth centuries. From this he deduced that by 1912 China was more than ripe for its French Revolution and therefore that Yüan Shih-k'ai's efforts to establish a new imperial dynasty would probably fail. Lest one naïvely suppose that Naitō was a liberal wishing the Chinese republicans well, I should add that he had a very poor opinion of republicanism as compared to aristocracy and an even poorer opinion of the opportunism of the Chinese govern-ing class. He clearly felt that strong inter-vention by the powers was called for in their own interests as well as in China's, especially in Manchuria where Japan should take the lead in keeping order.

It is of course unfair to criticize a theory solely on the basis of its motivation. One ought to take any rational arguments seri-ously and to judge the evidence on its merits. It is, however, extremely difficult in a case of this kind, where all depends on whether one can or cannot agree with the subjective opinion of the author of the theory that a historical situation in China and a similar situation elsewhere show "essentially" the same "stage of de-velopment," to know what counts as evi-dence or proof. In such circumstances one cannot help suspecting that nonrational factors may have had some part to play in the development of the theory. Still, others have independently held the view that the Sung dynasty corresponded in some essential way to the beginnings of what we term "modern" in the West and I shall return presently to this question.

In order to round off his theory Naitō had to provide a division between the ancient and medieval periods as well. In his first discussion of the problem he dealt only cursorily with this aspect of the matter and seems to have accepted the traditional schoolbook division which placed it at the unification of China by Ch'in in 221 B.C. Later he preferred to make the division at the end of the third century A.D. when North China fell under barbarian rule, thus drawing a parallel with the fall of the Roman Empire in the West. I should say that Naitō did not admit that he was simply drawing an analogy with the West but tried to establish rational criteria for his periodization from Chinese history itself.

Naitō's pupil and successor at Kyoto University, Professor Miyazaki Ichisada, has developed this theory further, attempting to strengthen the base in economic and social terms and to extend it into a general theory of world history. It is widely accepted in non-Marxist sinological circles in Japan (although there are a good many scholars who hold aloof), and has even had some influence on post-war Marxist thinking there.

Marxist theorizing about Chinese history has been going on hotly in the West, in Russia, in China and in Japan ever since about 1925. The focus of argument was at first the question of what exactly was meant by "Asiatic mode of production." Madyar in Russia took the view, which seems to be most easily justified on the basis of the canonical scriptures, that it was a special type of social structure peculiar to the Orient, characterized by lack of private ownership of land, large-scale public works, especially connected with irrigation, vil-

lage communes and despotism. It is essentially this theory that Dr. K. A. Wittfogel developed in Germany and later in America. It did not prove popular however in the Far East, since it seemed to carry the implication that Far Eastern history was innately stagnant and unprogressive and it was soon rejected in practical revolutionary politics. In 1927 the Central Committee of the Chinese Communist Party proclaimed that it was combating Asiatic society. The next year this was revised to read "feudal." Similarly Dr Kuo Mo-jo, whose theories are now orthodox in China, at first said that China was in a state of primitive society (which, as we have seen, was equivalent to Asiatic society in the writings of Marx and Engels); but he soon changed his mind and saw the same series of progressive stages in Chinese history as in the Marxist view of Western history. The theoretical question remained of how to interpret Marx's "Asiatic mode of production." It would be tedious to attempt to go over all the solutions proposed. The most commonly held view nowadays seems to be that it was a special form of slave society at the beginning of class society. The concept of Oriental despotism is sometimes separated off from it as a political form which existed along with various basic types of economic order in society.

If it was admitted that China had not been a peculiar, stagnant form of human society, then the next problem was to plot out the periods in her development. The most varied solutions have been proposed to this question by Marxists and those under Marxist influence. Some Chinese writers who have regarded the so-called feudal political organization of the Chou dynasty as equivalent to European feudalism have placed the end of the slave period anywhere from 1500 to 1000 B.C. This political so-called "feudalism" broke down in the Warring States period (fourth and third centuries B.C.) and there has been much controversy as to what was the stage reached by the new form of society that emerged from it. Any solution was bound to produce difficulties. If one said that it was an early stage of capitalism, as some did, then why had not the later forms of capitalism developed? Moreover, was it not a feudal society that the Chinese Communist Party was fighting against? The generally accepted solution has been to say that feudalism continued under a different form of political structure.

The most rigorous Marxist thinkers, alike in Russia, China and Japan, have rejected the identification of the political so-called "feudalism" of the first millennium B.C. with the economic form of society which, according to them, is properly denoted by that term. Present-day Russian opinion seems to be that China was a slave society until about the third or fourth century A.D. when the economic structure of society became feudal. From the beginning to the end, however, it remained imprisoned in the political form of Oriental despotism. Kuo Mo-jo's present view is that slave society gave way to feudal somewhere around 500 B.C., that is, when political "feudalism" was about to break down. In Japan since the war a divergent opinion first propounded by the late Maeda Naonori has become very generally accepted. This view stresses the unity of Far Eastern culture as a whole, including Korea, Japan and Annam[1] as well as China, and tries to find a periodization which will be roughly in step for all these countries. Maeda accepted Naitō Torajirō's view that a major break had occurred in Chinese history between T'ang and Sung, that is, around 1000 A.D., but reinterpreted this break as signifying the change from ancient (i.e. slave) society to medieval (i.e. feudal) society, where Naitō had seen it as the beginning of the modern age. So we find that the beginnings of feudalism have been placed on the one hand, as early as 1500 B.C. and, on the other hand, as late as 1000 A.D. with various intermediate points in between also chosen in one system or another. I should add that it is generally agreed among

Marxists that China came to the end of her strictly feudal period at the time of the Opium War (1839–42) and that a period of semi-feudalism, semi-colonialism, semi-capitalism followed until the Communist revolution of 1948.

The theoretical approaches to Chinese history that I have been discussing, all fall under the heading of what Professor K. R. Popper calls historicism.[2] They all assume that human history has everywhere followed a common organic pattern of development. Some think of the whole of history as a single organism; others think of it as a series or family of organisms, called "cultures" or "civilizations." Some think of the pattern of development as proceeding according to a rational dialectical principle; others merely point to the patterns without attempting to explain them — or they may appeal to poetry or myth by way of explanation. Professor Popper has thoroughly disposed of the claims of this general type of theory to be taken seriously and I shall certainly not attempt to improve on his arguments. I should only like to observe that the extreme divergency of the interpretations that have been imposed on Chinese history even by those claiming to accept the same scientific hypothesis, namely Marxism, would in any case suggest that something is radically wrong with the whole method.

Yet, if I reject not only the specific historicist theories that have been advanced to explain the course of Chinese history but also the whole approach which leads to such theories, I seem to have brought myself into a contradiction. For I began by demanding that we in the West should try to incorporate Chinese history into our picture of world history and by lamenting the way in which orthodox academic historians habitually ignore it. I am sure it is partly because of the urgent necessity which Far

[1] Roughly Vietnam. [Editor's note]

[2] "The poverty of historicism," *Economica* (1944), Vol. 11, pp. 86–103, 119–37 and (1945), Vol. 12, pp. 69–89. [Published also as a book by the Beacon Press (Boston, 1957). Editor's note.]

Eastern peoples have felt, to show that their own history is not something different in kind and separate from the history of the Western peoples, so much of whose civilization they have perforce had to adopt, that historicist theories have had such an appeal for them. Is it possible to satisfy this need in a legitimate way without building on such spurious and dangerous foundations?

If we insist on looking for a simple formula that will explain everything, I am afraid we shall not find it; but if we will have the patience and perseverance to study Chinese history in its sources with the thoroughness and care that we expect in other scholarly disciplines, if we do this not in a narrow spirit of pedantry but with our minds alert to the perennial problems that have assailed mankind everywhere — the basic biological urges of hunger and sex, the struggle with a grudging earth for the means of livelihood, the inadequacies of established social patterns to deal with new conditions, the oppression of the weak by the strong and the reaction of men driven to desperation, the universal aesthetic and religious aspirations of mankind, the problems of power and corruption — if we do this with imagination, but with imagination that will not go beyond what can be verified by evidence, we shall, I am sure, find that Chinese history throws light on our own history in countless ways and that mankind is indeed one. . . .

SUGGESTIONS FOR ADDITIONAL READING

Many books and articles on Chinese history fit their subject into periodic divisions or assign it a periodic character implicitly. No attempt will be made here to list such works. What follows are works that propose, describe, or discuss periodization explicitly. Acknowledgment should first be made, however, of the most recent contribution to a world history into which Chinese history might fall, namely, William H. McNeill, *The Rise of the West: A History of the Human Community* (Chicago, University of Chicago Press, 1963).

Among comprehensive schemes, the terms of the T'ang historian Liu Chih-chi are given by E. G. Pulleyblank in "Chinese Historical Criticism: Liu Chih-chi and Ssu-ma Kuang," in W. G. Beasley and E. G. Pulleyblank, eds., *Historians of China and Japan* (London, 1961), pp. 148–149. A summary of the Naitō hypothesis is given in Hisayuki Miyakawa, "An Outline of the Naitō Hypothesis and Its Effects on Japanese Studies of China," *Far Eastern Quarterly*, Vol. XIV, No. 4 (August 1955), pp. 533–552. A sympathetic description and elaboration in cultural spheres of J. S. Lee's cycle of internecine wars is in Lin Yutang, *My Country and My People* (New York, 1935), pp. 28–34. In honor of the memory of H. T. Lei, James T. C. Liu has written a note on periodization, proposing to divide history at about the point of the Naitō hypothesis, between "traditional" and "neo-traditional" periods. This should appear in the *Journal of Asian Studies* in 1964–65. The genesis of the dynastic cycle in its modern form may be traced from K. A. Wittfogel, "The Foundations and Stages of Chinese Economic History," *Zeitschrift für Sozialforschung*, No. IV (Paris, 1935), pp. 26–60. This also presents an early opinion of Professor Wittfogel on the establishment of Oriental despotism. The cycle is predicated by Wang Yü-ch'üan in "The Rise of Land Tax and the Fall of Dynasties in Chinese History," *Pacific Affairs*, Vol. IX, No. 2 (June 1936), pp. 201–220. Although Wang discusses mainly tax assessment and payment in the latter part of the Ch'ing dynasty, his thesis aims at more general validity. Another statement of the dynastic cycle appears in Owen Lattimore, *Inner Asian Frontiers of China* (Boston, 1962), pp. 45, 46, and 531ff. This discussion includes remarks on the patterns of J. S. Lee and Chi Ch'ao-ting. Mr. Lattimore also proposes interaction between a Chinese cycle and a steppe cycle. According to recent word of mouth, however, he may no longer hold the views in his book. The dynastic cycle, it should be added, faces attack. Professor Hans H. A. Bielenstein, for instance, proposes to include a refutation of the thesis of a cycle in the Han dynasties in a new book.

Among prominent Western sinologists, Henri Maspero left a chart arranged periodically in *Mélanges posthumes sur les religions et l'histoire de la Chine* (Paris, 1950), Vol. III, pp. 231–233. Unfortunately there appears to be no discussion of the periodization.

Reviews and criticisms of several schemes include Meribeth E. Cameron, "Periodization of Chinese History," *Pacific Historical Review*, Vol. XV, No. 2 (June 1946), pp. 171–177. She comments on the dynastic cycle, K. A. Wittfogel, Owen Lattimore, Ch'ao-ting Chi, H. T. Lei, A. Toynbee, and Lin Mou-sheng. Wolfram Eberhard discusses other theories than his own, especially K. A. Wittfogel's, in Chapter Two of *Conquerors and Rulers: Social Forces in Medieval China* (Leiden, 1952). Periodization within the Communist premises, especially in China since 1949, is critically reviewed in Albert Feuerwerker, "China's History in Marxian Dress," *Ameri-*

can Historical Review, Vol. LXVI, No. 2 (January 1961), pp. 323–353. Benjamin Schwartz discusses one aspect of the background of Marxian periodization disputes — the attempt to explain the nature of modern, pre-Communist Chinese society — in "A Marxist Controversy on China," *Far Eastern Quarterly,* No. XIII (1954), pp. 143–153. A response in Communist mode to the criticisms of E. G. Pulleyblank is in Jaroslav Průšek, "Some Chinese Studies," *Archiv Orientální,* Vol. XXVII, No. 3 (1959), pp. 481–483.

On the whole, periodization of Chinese history seems to have received more attention from Japanese and Chinese writers than European and American in recent years. Some of the Oriental discussion has been briefly summarized or listed in "Literature on the Chinese Soviet Movement," (Pacific Affairs Bibliographies No. III) *Pacific Affairs,* Vol. IX, No. 3 (September 1936), pp. 421–435; Akira Fujieda and Wilma Fairbank, "Current Trends in Japanese Studies of China and Adjacent Areas," *Far Eastern Quarterly,* No. XIII (1953),

pp. 37–47; Albert Feuerwerker and S. Cheng, *Chinese Communist Studies of Modern Chinese History* (Cambridge, Mass., 1961), pp. 21–27; John King Fairbank and Masataka Banno, *Japanese Studies of Modern China* (Harvard-Yenching Institute, 1955), pp. 17–24; and Gotō Kimpei, "Postwar Japanese Studies on Chinese Social and Economic History," *Monumenta Serica,* No. 17 (1958), pp. 377–418. The last of these comments especially is on the division among Japanese scholars between followers of the Naitō proposal and that of Maeda Naonori.

Readers of Chinese and Japanese might begin their examination of modern discussions by consulting Yao Tsung-wu, *Tungpei shih lun-tsung* (Taipei, 1959), pp. 1–26. This reviews and discusses several modern Chinese theories from that of Liang Ch'i-ch'ao forward but ignores the major historical-materialist views. For those in both China and Japan, as well as for other important Japanese schemes, see Suzuki Shun's essay on periodization in *Ajia rekishi jiten* (Tokyo, 1959–1962), IV: 168–170.